DAVE THOMAS

WITH DAVID ROBERTS

GUIDING ME
HOME & AWAY

THE AUTOBIOGRAPHY

Dave Thomas: Guiding Me Home & Away
Published 2019 by Hornet Books
Text © Dave Thomas 2019
This Work © Hornet Books Ltd
ISBN 978-0-9957658-7-0

This book is also available as an ebook and in formats for blind and partially sighted readers. Contact Hornet Books for further details.

The publishers have made every reasonable effort to trace the copyright owners of photographs used in this book. In the event of an omission or error, the publishers will be pleased to hear from anyone who has not been appropriately acknowledged and rectify any issues in future reprints and editions.

Proofreader: Matthew White

Hornet Books
Ground Floor, 2B Vantage Park, Washingley Road,
Huntingdon, PE29 6SR

www.hornetbooks.com

info@hornetbooks.com

For Brenda &
Mum & Dad

INTRODUCTION

In 2008, former England international footballer Dave Thomas went for a driver's field of vision test. It wasn't the first time he'd been examined. Dave's eyesight wasn't all it should be and his PE teacher job involved a good deal of driving school teams back and forth. Dave was worried.

Acknowledging the authorities had a very strict criteria, Dave was still unprepared for the shock he received one morning in September that year.

Dave's wife Brenda heard the postman's delivery and picked up the letters from the mat, joking to him as she called out: "More fan mail for you David!"

Brenda's daily jibe was only half said in jest. The ex-Burnley, QPR and Everton winger continues to enjoy a good few letters from fans and even visits from the occasional one or two, who roll up at his rural home in County Durham.

But among the pile of letters that day was a brown envelope from the DVLA that Dave had to admit was life-changing. It spelt out in no uncertain terms that he was to cease driving immediately.

These days, 'registered blind' is a fact he has had to come to terms with, or, as Dave would say, "adapt to".

Anyone who knows him well will attest to Dave's incredibly positive attitude to life, and in the numerous press and TV interviews he has done since his sight deteriorated he insists that he accepted the devastating news immediately.

Despite many tearful moments relating the difficult issues that come with progressive sight loss and the more emotional parts of his story, the ever-positive Dave always avoids putting a negative spin on this setback.

Someone who sees things a little differently is Brenda. She witnessed at first hand a man losing more than just his driving licence, and after one dramatic incident at Epsom racecourse she broached the subject: "David, I think we should look into how it might be possible to get you a guide dog."

Without giving too much of his story away - there's a guide dog on the cover of this book after all! - Dave was eventually paired with Hannah and began a new independent and confident life.

He's had to make some astonishing changes to his life: the first half packed with incredible footballing drama before encountering the wonderful people he has got to know as a result of his blindness in the second.

This book is clearly more than just another footballer's autobiography. Working with Dave has been an uplifting and inspirational experience.

We hope some of Dave's infectious positive formula for life rubs off on the pages that follow.

David Roberts & Bob Young - Hornet Books

CHAPTER 1

Grandad Wins the World Cup!

Although I'd always say to anyone I'm from the north-east and proud of it, I was actually born in Nottinghamshire. My mother's family were from that area and I was born in the small market town of Kirkby-in-Ashfield, which was once well-known for mining and as a railway hub. The town's most famous son was cricketing great Harold Larwood, who people of a certain generation will remember for the legendary "bodyline" Ashes series.

Born on the 5th of October 1950, I didn't stay in Nottinghamshire for long. It was only a matter of a few weeks before mum Jessie, dad David Lloyd and me upped sticks and moved to the north-east. Our destination was the mining village of West Auckland in County Durham, where we moved into my dad's parents' house.

Incredibly, my father lived in the same house in West Auckland for 94 years, the same house his father (my grandad) had lived in before him. And that's where I was brought up, along with my brother Melvin, who arrived on the scene ten years later in 1960. Our home was on Staindrop Road, in a property that is still standing today, which was owned by the Thomas family up until 2015, when my mum moved out to live in residential care.

Football played a big part in my early family life. My dad - always called Lloyd, never David - was a goalkeeper playing locally for Shildon Bridge Railway. He began his working life as a miner, but became a welder for British Rail for 42 years at what they called Shildon Shops, where they made railway wagons.

Not surprisingly, the Thomas family had very strong Welsh connections. Grandad David's middle name was Reece - a very Welsh name. It was grandad who was a big influence on me and my football. He was 73 when I was born and he encouraged me enormously until he died in 1963, when I was just 13. He'd take me out to a field at the back of our house with a ball and his coaching was simple. As I was a natural right-footer he'd tell me, "You've got to kick with your left foot." If I resisted he'd say, "Right - I'm going in", which he'd then pretend to do. Through him persisting with that mantra, day after day, I've since then always been able to kick with both feet. Crucially, it meant I would always be comfortable playing on the left wing or right wing.

Recently, I was looking through an old copy of the *Northern Echo*, in which mum and dad were quoted, saying how grandad's coaching had made such an impact on me. I'd forgotten that I'd played for the local under-11 side St Helens when I was only seven years old. Nicknamed "The Mighty Midgets", that team only lost once in four years according to mum.

Although grandad had never played football professionally, he had one massive claim to fame. One of the best amateur players in the 1890s, he turned out for Bishop Auckland and West Auckland as a midfielder, or half-back as they used to call them back then. He'd come from the Stoke-on-Trent area and got the secretary's job at one of the local pits when he headed north-east. Because he didn't want to uproot his wife and family, he turned down an offer to coach football in Italy. He did play football on the continent at one point though, and featured in one of the most improbable footballing stories of all time.

Grandad's remarkable adventure began when wealthy Scotsman Sir Thomas Lipton, famous as the Lipton tea man, put up the money for a football tournament abroad. West Auckland Football Club were, at the time, a great amateur side made up mostly of miners, and they bizarrely represented England in Turin in 1909, in what has become known famously as the first football World Cup. Sir Thomas donated a beautiful, huge, solid-silver trophy for the competition and, against all the odds, West Auckland won it after beating top club sides representing Germany, Italy and Switzerland. And my grandad was captain, so you can imagine how proud I am. That team of coal miners travelled by train, bus and boat there and back to Italy - quite a feat in those days.

The story becomes even more incredible when you think that the Football Association at the time wanted no part in Sir Thomas Lipton's project. The mystery as to why West Auckland Football Club were ever invited to play is said to be due to the FA originally declining an opportunity to send Woolwich Arsenal Football Club to the event, and West Auckland taking their place as their initials were the same as those of the prestigious London club.

Despite West Auckland's success, they had an immediate problem while they were over in Italy. My grandad and the rest of the team ran out of money and couldn't get home. Stuck at

Turin railway station, they sent a telegram to the landlady of a pub in Shildon, who promised she'd put the money up for the lads' return fare as long as she could have the cup on display in the pub. And that's exactly what happened. The cup was in the Eden Arms for 50 odd years. Subsequently, the local working men's club in West Auckland raised funds to buy the cup so it could be displayed there, where it stayed until 1994, when it was stolen. It was never seen again, so the cup that now has pride of place at the town's football club is a replica.

In 1911, two years after that first tournament in Italy, West Auckland returned to defend their trophy and won the thing again, thrashing Juventus 6-1 in the final.

In 1982, a film depicting this incredible story was released. In *The World Cup - A Captain's Tale*, actor and football fan Dennis Waterman starred alongside Tim Healy, Richard Griffiths and Nigel Hawthorne in what turned out to be a popular and critical success. My grandad, 'Ticer' Thomas, was played by David 'Dai' Bradley, the young Yorkshire actor famous for his starring role as Billy Casper in the 1969 film *Kes*.

Just as well my grandad had left behind a little notebook of all the events during the tournament in Italy. Thankfully, my father had kept the book safe. It proved invaluable when Tyne Tees Television, who were attempting to produce the film, came to our house. Borrowing the book and grandad's World Cup-winning medal, they took both with them to show the Italians, who had little or no record of the 1909 competition in their archives. The TV producer even slept with grandad's medal round her neck when she had it in her possession as it was obviously quite collectible. I don't think the film would ever have been made if it wasn't for dad's help in letting Tyne Tees have grandad's old ready reckoner containing all that information.

Sadly, there was a certain amount of discontent and aggro in the family when it came to distributing grandad's possessions after he passed away. My father, because he'd looked after my grandad for all those years, had his football memorabilia - FA Amateur Cup winner's medal, Northern League winner's medal and World Cup winner's medal - kept in a cabinet in our house. Dad had two brothers and two sisters, and when the film came out all those years later my uncle Harry, who lived down in Southend-on-Sea, rang my dad and said "That's my medal!" My dad was so upset he posted it to his brother in an envelope with no letter.

It got there, but to this day I have no idea where that medal is now.

And that's the story of David 'Ticer' Thomas, so called because he was not just a useful footballer but also a fantastic cricketer. He was a spin bowler and apparently he used to "tice" the ball, to use the cricketing jargon, on to the wicket.

One final thing about *The World Cup - A Captain's Tale*: I was lucky enough to meet Dennis Waterman years later on a golf trip, and he thought it was one of the best dramas he'd worked on. He'd started the whole idea of a film when he'd read a newspaper article about West Auckland winning the World Cup and pitched it to some of his contacts in the film industry.

These days, there's a magnificent three-metre-high bronze statue commemorating the wonderful achievement of those miners opposite West Auckland Working Men's Club. I had the great honour of unveiling the statue, along with actor Tim Healy and Sir John Hall. It was a proud moment and, as I said at the ceremony that damp October afternoon in 2013, "Grandad would have loved this statue."

Tim Healy, who played the part of Charlie Hogg in *A Captain's*

Tale, said it was the acting role that launched his career, winning him a part in the hit TV series *Auf Wiedersehen, Pet*.

"It was the bestest job I ever had," he told the crowd that day. "Thirteen lads going to Italy to play football and getting paid for it. I want to thank West Auckland. Every time I drive by that statue I cry 'YES!'"

Fittingly, the statue, which was sculptured by Nigel Boonham and cost more than £170,000, includes a footballer and a miner. Both figures appear to be based on one particular face in the West Auckland team photos of the time, and it's not just me who believes that the face is that of 'Ticer' Thomas.

If you want to see the statue, just head to the West Auckland Working Men's Club on Front Street. West Auckland Town FC, as they are now known, are based just a few hundred yards away, and that's where the replica Thomas Lipton trophy is displayed. Nice to see that the story lives on: even the club badges on the shirts of the current West Auckland Town team depict that famous trophy.

A lovely postscript to this story: that original World Cup trophy might have been pressed into action again in 1966, when the Jules Rimet Trophy was stolen. The Sir Thomas Lipton Trophy was earmarked as a replacement until Pickles the dog famously found the Jules Rimet cup wrapped in newspaper under a hedge. Those familiar pictures of Bobby Moore holding the World Cup aloft in 1966 might have looked quite different but for Pickles' intervention.

CHAPTER 2
One Pound Six and Eight Pence

had a wonderful childhood. We were a tight-knit family. Christmases were particularly special and mostly hosted by mum's sister down in Hucknall, Nottinghamshire. Auntie Min knew how to organise Christmas, and with another seven sisters in the family there was always quite a squeeze around the table. Like a lot of boys, I was lucky enough to get the Christmas present of my dreams one year. A Hornby train set. Down the stairs I tumbled one Christmas morning to find the whole set expertly spread out around the living room floor ready for me to play with. A kind labour of love, no doubt, for my dad and uncle. Looking back now, I bet the two of them enjoyed playing with it just as much as I did. They must have been up quite late that Christmas Eve!

My school days were, on the whole, enjoyable. When the big change from primary to secondary school came, I coped with it pretty well I think. I passed the first half of my 11+ exam but failed the second part so I went to Barnard Castle Secondary Modern School, which was about 12 miles from home. I got on well with all who taught me aside from my science teacher, who was vicious to everyone and should never have been a teacher. Mr Hartley had a terrible temper and I made sure I never got on the wrong side of him.

If I wasn't playing football, the other sport I really enjoyed was cricket and I played for a team in the Durham Senior League when I was only 14. So, what with my schoolwork, there wasn't much time for anything else. But what little time I did have left after lessons or sporting activities I'd occasionally spend acting in the school plays. I really loved that. The teachers in charge of drama were Miss Collins and Miss Watson. Lovely they were. They'd give me time off to play football as long as I rehearsed when I could and learned my lines. One school production that sticks out in my memory was a play called *The Parker Plan*. Somehow, my mate Michael Taylor and I managed to bag the leading roles of Horace and Willie and we both thoroughly enjoyed the experience. Michael still lives in the Barnard Castle area and I was gobsmacked to meet him out of the blue one day recently after a 50-year gap. He immediately recalled our great acting partnership!

So far, this is maybe creating an image of the perfect schoolboy and I certainly wasn't that. Academically I was okay at maths, but apart from that no great shakes at English and much else. I wouldn't say I misbehaved much, but enough to get caned by the headmaster twice. The first occasion was for fighting and the second for pitching a golf ball through a window, which I suppose is fair enough. I couldn't really complain, could I?

I was fortunate to have two very good PE teachers. The first was Sid Bainbridge, but he moved on to be replaced by a guy called Don Sparks. Mr Sparks was a fantastic amateur footballer who played for Bishop Auckland and Crook Town, won the FA Amateur Cup, and I think he may have played for England Amateurs. As you can imagine, the amount of time he gave me helped me greatly. I enjoyed my football so much and he promoted me a lot and pushed me to get trials. Perhaps surprisingly I never played for a boy's club, just the school, and that was how I was spotted by a scout, which began the process which would see me eventually sign for Burnley Football Club.

My father never missed a match during the time I played all over County Durham. He took me everywhere in a motorbike and sidecar. I even remember the registration, TUP 438, all these years later! It was a BSA Golden Flash 650cc: funny how you remember these things. On cold winter days, my mother used to put a hot water bottle in the sidecar for me. Dad couldn't drive a car, but he never missed a game. He always wanted a Reliant Robin because, as it was a three-wheeler, he wouldn't need to pass his test.

Mum also attended games when she could, and the support from both of them was so important. They were wonderful parents and gave up so much for me. During all my school years, mum would always be up before me to chop wood and get the fire lit every morning before I left on the long trek to school. Mind you, I was hardly at home. If I wasn't playing football, I'd be watching it. Our two local teams of note, Bishop Auckland and West Auckland, were the teams my grandad had played for. Despite the fact that they were amateur football clubs, both were decent teams back in the '50s when I was growing up. Bishop Auckland were the dominant local team during that decade and won the FA Amateur Cup three seasons running in 1956, 1957 and 1958. Then, across town, West Auckland FC were Northern

League champions in 1959-60, Northern League Cup winners the same season and again in 1962-63, and FA Amateur Cup finalists at Wembley in 1960-61.

Apart from obviously watching the final at home on TV with my family, my earliest memories of the FA Cup came from watching West Auckland as a schoolboy. West Auckland FC held a particular place in my heart of course, because of grandad's World Cup victory. A vivid FA Cup memory came in a game that never concluded. I think they were playing Walton & Hersham in midweek and I remember running down to the ground from my home about 800 yards away and West Auckland were getting beat. There had been a tremendous amount of rain that particular week, and at the back of the field, even today, there's a beck - a small river - and the fields were flooded and one or two of the supporters allegedly dug under the foundations of the brick perimeter with spades and let the water come pouring in. It had the desired effect. As a result, the game was abandoned! West Auckland went on to win the re-arranged replay, which again I dashed home from school to see. Just to add to this bizarre story, quite by chance I met a guy at the local golf club recently called Keith Walker, who lived and worked locally in Barnard Castle back in those days. It turned out he was at that same abandoned FA Cup match and reassured me it was all true and I hadn't dreamt it.

As I've said, I didn't have many free Saturdays from playing football to be a spectator. And in those days, remember, there was no professional football played on Sundays. As a consequence I didn't see enough games to call myself a supporter of any of the local professional clubs. But when the opportunity arose, my dad and I would make the trip to Ayresome Park to see Middlesbrough. This was at a time when Brian Clough was rattling in the goals for them. As I recall, they were a team always in the top half of League Division 2 [now the Championship] back when I was a lad. I don't remember much about 'Cloughie', although he will pop up later in my story. One player I do remember dad pointing out to me was a Northern Ireland lad called Peter McParland. Playing against the Boro for Aston Villa one Saturday afternoon, McParland was mesmerising. The reason I recall him even now was simple. He was a winger. Perhaps dad was educating me in the finer points of wing play. Anyway, McParland was exceptional that day and possibly something of a role model.

Another potential role model for me was Stanley Matthews. Sadly, I never got to see him play. Dad did take both of us in the motorbike and sidecar one Saturday to Roker Park to take in a Sunderland versus Stoke City match in which Sir Stan was due to play for the visitors. Two things conspired to make it a wasted journey. Dad parked the motorbike and sidecar a fair distance from the ground, but it became evident that a sizeable crowd was descending on Roker Park. Maybe others had the idea that it might be a last chance to see the great man play. Anyway, the attendance was massive that day and we couldn't get in the ground. As it turned out, had we passed through the turnstiles we wouldn't have seen the legendary winger play after all: Matthews, as was the case a fair amount in the twilight of his career, was injured that day, and not selected to play.

I did enjoy those trips out with dad though. Football attendances were booming back in the post-war period and I got a real buzz watching a game as a lad among thousands of people. Back then, adults and children were often separated in those vast crowds. At Middlesbrough, dad would head for the terraces but I'd be in a junior paddock, which made me a bit wary. Looking back, it's incredible to think that both Middlesbrough and Sunderland were playing in the Second Division with such big crowds watching them. My region was a hotbed of football, a fact acknowledged when Ayresome Park, Middlesbrough, was selected as one of the venues for the forthcoming 1966 FIFA World Cup. Little did I realise at the time that the excitement and noise generated by such passionate north-east crowds would be something I would experience first-hand as a professional footballer just a few years later.

So, my experience of life as a football fanatic didn't stretch geographically much further than Sunderland and Middlesbrough. I never ventured far enough north to watch Newcastle United at St James' Park. And culturally my experiences of anything else didn't stretch much beyond occasional visits to my cinema in West Auckland. Unsurprisingly, the film that had the most profound effect on me was the Hammer horror movie *The Revenge of Frankenstein*. I was far too young to have honestly gained entry for what, in those days, must surely have been an 'X'-rated film. Not that Peter Cushing and co. left an indelible impression. The only people left properly horrified must have been my fellow cinema-goers in the seats in front of me and my mates. I vividly remember screwing up pieces of paper into tight balls and projecting them at some speed into their necks with the aid of our rubber-band catapults.

When I wasn't catapulting, I was firing off arrows. Our favourite outdoor pursuit, apart from football, was our own West Auckland version of 'Cowboys and Indians' - or was it Robin Hood? Anyway, we fashioned our own home-made bows and arrows from the local woodlands and hedgerows. Great fun during the long summer school holidays.

I did go to music lessons. However, it was very difficult finding the time for that knowing I wanted to play football. I didn't have to go far for those lessons. Miss Heslop was my piano teacher and she lived just a couple of hundred yards from my home. She was lovely, but quite demanding. I practised, but whether enough to call myself a musician I'm not quite sure. My love of playing music I inherited from my father. Dad was a pianist but also a wonderful cornet player who performed in the Royal Engineers band during wartime. I think I got to grade 2 in my piano-playing before football took up all my time.

Unlike a lot of kids who may have had a paper round or ran errands for pocket money, I never really had time for a part-time job. In fact, the only money I earned before my football career took off was the princely sum of one pound six and eight pence! That £1, six shillings and 8 pence sticks in my mind as if it was earned yesterday. It was the sum total of my own little business initiative using my musical ability as a 13-year-old. That Christmas, in 1963, I went door to door round our neighbourhood playing Christmas carols on my dad's piano accordion. The money seemed like a fortune to me at the time. I'd knock on doors in the pitch-black thinking I'll have to get these bellows going ready for when the door opens! It wasn't the easiest thing to play - buttons on the left-hand side and a keyboard on the right - but I must have done okay. The response from the neighbours was pretty good. Those piano lessons stood me in good stead though. I still love playing to this day.

Not all of our neighbours appreciated my football skills quite so much. Next door were Mr and Mrs Whitfield, who were lovely, but our other immediate neighbours in Staindrop Road, Mr and Mrs Ward, weren't nearly so nice. When kicking a ball in our back yard, if it went over in to their back yard it would never ever return. The ball, we were told in no uncertain terms, went on the fire!

I'm ashamed to say that one of the great passions we had as boys back then was collecting wild birds' eggs. This was a hobby that got me into trouble in a way you might not expect. I was perhaps about ten or eleven. There was a terraced street in West Auckland where my best friend Neil Salt used to live with his mum and his sister. Ironically, the street was called New Street. Ironic because all the old houses were being demolished one by one in what was quite a rough area, and all the residents were gradually moving out. Me, Neil, and another friend of ours called Tony Jarvis, climbed up into this attic in one of the empty houses looking for pigeon eggs. The attics had no partitions between each terraced house, so it was all one long, enormous space.

Tony cried out to me, "Make sure you stand on the joists - don't tread anywhere else."

What did I do? I missed my footing and went straight through the bloody ceiling. There I was, hanging on to the joist with my legs dangling. And there's an elderly man and woman in bed below me having an afternoon kip! What a mess. The pigeon eggs all ended up on the bed with most of the bits of plaster, and I just about managed to haul myself up before all three of us boys legged it. I didn't dare tell mum and dad, at least not for weeks after.

I got into even worse trouble with an incident a while later. This time I can honestly say I was innocent of pretty much any blame. But it wasn't an experience I'll forget in a hurry. Not funny in the slightest, this time.

Once again, I was out and about with Neil. My aunt and uncle lived at Tindall Crescent, where there was a nearby railway goods yard with old carriages and guards vans. Neil and I were visiting one Sunday, and we went down to the yard and knocked on the door of the hut at the depot, where two guys looking after the place were playing cards. I asked one of them, "Hope you don't mind me asking but could we have a look round?"

The guy looked up from his cards and said, "Yeah - get yourselves round there."

So off Neil and I went to explore. While we were on one of the old carriages, a railway policeman appeared and asked us what we thought we were doing. He took us back to the hut where the guys were playing cards and they denied ever having given us permission to look round.

Neil and I were both prosecuted for trespassing.

We had to go to the magistrates' court in Bishop Auckland and it all got rather expensive, particularly for my mum and dad. Having been prosecuted, my dad had to cough up for fines for me and for Neil, as Neil's dad wasn't around at the time. I was really affected by the whole affair. It was a nervous period while we waited for the court appearance to come around. We were only eleven at the time.

It was far safer and less stressful playing football!

CHAPTER 3
Signing for Burnley

As you will know by now, the Thomas' were a real footballing family. Grandad in particular and dad had their moments, and although my younger brother Melvin never made it professionally, he did have a trial at Wolves. We all enjoyed our football and played the game regularly, and it came as a nice surprise when I began to realise I might be the one to make a career from it.

Before I signed schoolboy forms for Burnley, I'd had trials with two of their Lancashire rivals. First up was Blackpool, who were a well-established top-division club at the time managed by a guy called Ron Suart. Dad accompanied me down to Lancashire. At the trial I remember seeing Alan Ball as a young kid, long before he got transferred to Everton. I would have been 12 years old back then in 1962 and Alan about five years older. Soon after that I went down to Preston North End. There was a hairdresser locally in Bishop Auckland called Jack Hailey who knew my dad, which led to my trial there. Even though they were a Second Division [now Championship] club, for some reason I remember I liked Preston more than Blackpool. Under guidance from my dad, I guess you could say we were playing the field. Dad didn't want to commit to either Blackpool or Preston and it was the third Lancashire club that immediately seemed to be the most attractive proposition.

On the day I was scouted by Burnley, I wasn't aware of the fact at all. The first I knew of any approach was when I was coming out of assembly at Barnard Castle School one morning. My religious education teacher, a man called Mr Charlton, was waiting for me. He was a lovely teacher, but he'd never kicked a football in his life. Mr Charlton pulled me to one side and said, "David, there's a man called Jack Robson trying to get in contact with you. I think he's a scout for Burnley Football Club."

Well, as you can imagine, in those days we had no telephone, so all I could do was give Mr Charlton mum and dad's address. Mr Charlton must have somehow dropped that slip of paper I gave him with the address on it off at Jack Robson's home in Darlington. As a result, Robson drove over to see my mum and dad and that's how I ended up going down to Burnley Football Club.

Jack Robson's uncle was a guy called Jack Hixon. Robson, Hixon and another man called George Murray were the big three football scouts in the north-east of England at the time. People could never understand how Newcastle United, Middlesbrough and Sunderland didn't nab some of the best north-east lads. The answer was simple: they nearly all went to Burnley! Hixon found numerous players: Ralph Coates, Brian O'Neil, John Angus - all north-east lads. There were more north-east lads at Burnley than from anywhere else and that's why, when I eventually made my way there, I felt comfortable. Not all the best north-east talent signed for Burnley. It was Jack Hixon who found Alan Shearer, who ended up at Southampton as a young kid.

Burnley's interest in me was, of course, flattering. Once I began playing for England Schoolboys I think that increased the interest from a number of other clubs, including Manchester United, but I happily signed for Burnley.

The manager at the time was Harry Potts. He was wonderful for Burnley. He had already guided the club to the League Championship - and a place in the European Cup - a few seasons back in 1959-60. Once scout Jack Robson had tipped off the club, Mr Potts came to see my dad and Mr Bailey, our headmaster at my school in Barnard Castle, so that I could sign my schoolboy forms.

To get the manager to come to Barnard Castle School was unique. It was an incredibly exciting time. All I wanted to do was play football. Could this be a career? People ask me all the time, 'What would you have been if you weren't a footballer?' and I honestly haven't a clue! My father worked hard, day shifts and night shifts, as a miner earlier in his life, then worked equally hard for British Rail. Lads quite often followed their dads down the pit back then, but there was just a chance my working career might turn out differently.

Signing schoolboy forms for Burnley didn't stop one final attempt by Leeds United to persuade us that I should join them. Their manager, Don Revie, was in the early stages of building a really great team at Elland Road that would go on to dominate English football in the early '70s. Apparently, I was on his shopping list.

He must have seen me or been aware of me playing for England Schoolboys but wanted a closer look at what I could do.

I was 15 and I'd just been playing in a Durham county match and dad had brought me home as usual.

I'd just played 80 minutes, and as soon as I walked in the door my mum called out, "Can you go and get me a loaf of bread?"

Now I lost my mum in 2018 - she was 97 when she passed away - but without fail, any time in our lives when my brother Melvin or I went to see her she'd always say, "Can you go to the shops and get me such and such."

And in 1965 I vividly remember this particular trip to the shop - Oxley's it was - for good reason. As I was walking up the street - and you can imagine there weren't many vehicles about back then - there was a car curb-crawling very slowly next to me on the pavement. As I walked a little bit quicker, it seemed as though the car did the same. Then it stopped and the window was wound down.

I called out, "Can I help you?" and as I looked inside the car I recognised the figure in the passenger seat. It was Don Revie.

In the driver's seat, as we later discovered, was his chief scout, and unbeknown to me they had been to the Durham county game I had played in earlier that day.

Revie said, "David Thomas?"

I said, "Yes."

He said, "I've been to watch you play and we followed you back on that motorbike and sidecar of yours." He then went on to say that he wanted to visit my mum and dad to talk to them.

"Where do you live?" he asked.

"Down there in that terraced house. No. 35," I replied, pointing. "But I'll have to get a loaf of bread first otherwise my mother'll tell us off."

So, I get the loaf and then go back home, followed by Revie and his chief scout. In the house they both come and we sit down in the front sitting room with mum, dad and Melvin. As mum pours them a cup of tea, Don Revie speaks.

"Mr Thomas," he says, "I've been watching your David play today and we'd like him to come down to Yorkshire and sign for Leeds United."

Straight away dad responds, "Canna do that. Impossible. David's just signed schoolboy forms for Burnley."

At that, Revie says, "Well I think he can sign for us. There are ways and means of getting around that."

I don't remember saying too much, but in any case dad was adamant that I was promised to Burnley. But Revie wasn't giving up.

Before he got up to leave he says, "If you don't mind I'll come back up to West Auckland in 48 hours and bring my chairman with me."

I was quite happy to go to Burnley and my dad wasn't budging, but what could we do to stop them? I don't think mum, dad, my brother or I actually expected Revie to come back, but we were wrong.

Two days later, I'm sorting through the post and I see through the front window there's a Rolls-Royce pulling up outside our house.

Almost immediately, out come the neighbours to have a look as in through the front door come Mr Revie and his chairman Mr Reynolds.

I'm absolutely bricking it, wondering what the heck is going on.

We sat down and Revie was quiet this time. Mr Reynolds did all the talking.

Again, the same proposal: "We'd like to sign your David as an apprentice at Leeds."

Again, the same answer from dad: "We canna do that. David's happy to go to Burnley. Aren't you David?"

"Yes dad," I replied.

Then there was a pause before Mr Reynolds spoke again.

"Mr Thomas. Do you mind me asking - how much is your David going to get a week at Burnley?"

Dad said proudly: "He's getting four pound basic and he's getting his digs paid for, so that would be worth about £8 total a week."

Another pause, then Mr Reynolds responds: "If we give your David £30 a week basic and pay his digs how would that be?"

Now dad wasn't earning that at the time, so anyone could see that this was a fantastic offer.

Before he could answer, Mr Reynolds reached down and pulled a briefcase on to his lap. He opened the case and tilted it forward in front of us.

The case was full of more money than we had ever seen in one place before. Inside was £2,000, all in brand-spanking-new £5 notes.

This was big money to us. I worked out that back in 1965 mum and dad's house was probably worth about five-hundred quid, so the contents of that case would probably have bought three or four houses in our terraced street.

But *still* dad wasn't budging.

"I'm a man of my word," dad said, "and David has to go to Burnley."

Well, Mr Reynolds knew that was it. But I'll never forget what he did next. He reached into the case and pulled off a fiver from the piles of banknotes and handed it to my brother.

Then he turned to dad and said, "I really admire your honesty Mr Thomas. I wish David well in his career."

And that was that.

After Revie and Reynolds had left, dad said, "I'm going to ask Burnley Football Club to up their wages!"

So next time we were down at Turf Moor, dad spoke to Albert Maddox, the dogmatic secretary at the football club, to arrange a meeting with the rather intimidating chairman, Bob Lord, or 'Bulldog' Bob Lord as we called him. It wasn't easy, but eventually dad got his meeting and straight away Bob Lord kicked things off with, "What do you want Mr Thomas?!"

Well, dad didn't dare tell Bob Lord about the Leeds approach - Bob Lord hated Leeds.

Dad just quietly went through all the positives about my England Schoolboys caps and all my various attributes and asked if it might be possible to have a signing-on fee.

Bob Lord repeated, "What do you want?"

So, dad said tentatively, "Would £500 be all right?"

To which Bob Lord instantly responded, "Yes. No trouble."

Afterwards, outside the chairman's office on the way out, dad turned to me and said quietly, "Blow me. If I'd asked for £2,000 he'd have probably given it to me!"

Albert Maddox duly gave dad the £500 and he opened a building society account in Bishop Auckland. Every week after that dad would pay an extra tenner into that account, just in case the tax man took some.

There were never any regrets about signing for Burnley. Not by me or by mum and dad.

Remember, Burnley had not so long ago won the league and, as champions, entered the European Cup [now the Champions League] the following season, a competition they took in their stride by finishing as quarter-finalists. All this was recent history when I joined them, but it wasn't just the on-field success that was impressive. The club looked after us really well and Harry Potts, it would become apparent later, had really good man-management skills, which suited me. Not only that, he had been born in the north-east, in Hetton-le-Hole, 20 miles or so from my West Auckland home. There were a lot of good omens.

Like most people lucky enough to have witnessed the England World Cup win, I have such vivid memories of 1966. Coincidentally, I was at home in my local town, West Auckland, when some of the group matches were played nearby at Middlesbrough's old ground that summer. Not only football fans but the whole of the north-east were excited by it, especially that shock result when North Korea beat Italy at Ayresome Park. Another powerful memory was a match I watched at home with mum and dad when Brazil played at Goodison Park, Everton, and Pelé got kicked to bits by the Portuguese. That was a key game as Brazil were beaten that night and Portugal's Eusébio went on to be one of the stars of the tournament. Obviously, all the Thomas family gathered round our little black-and-white TV to watch the England v West Germany Wembley final, but in all honesty, at the age I was then, I was probably more interested in playing than watching even big games like that.

The funny thing was, I'd actually played at Wembley earlier that year for England Schoolboys against West Germany, so you can see why it was such a vivid, exciting time in my life. From April, all the way through to England winning the World Cup, it was such a special spring and summer for me. We played Northern Ireland, Wales, Scotland and West Germany. Obviously playing football at school in the north-east, you played for your district area, which was Bishop Auckland Boys, and then if you were lucky enough you were selected to play for the county - County Durham - and then went for trials. At those trials you would have a team from the north and a team from the south, and in my case that final trial game was at Vicarage Road, Watford Football Club. You hope to get selected and I was fortunate enough to get picked for the national squad.

My England Schoolboys team played Northern Ireland in Birmingham, Wales at York, and West Germany at Wembley. I think whenever I sum up my football career, that period was probably one of the biggest highlights. Fifteen years old, representing my country at schoolboy international level, I'd signed for Burnley Football Club on schoolboy forms and the future looked really bright for me.

Mum and dad were so supportive during my young teenage years. They somehow managed to always be there for me when I was playing or travelling to games. It was nice that they were so well looked after themselves now that I'd signed for Burnley. The club put them up in a hotel in London when I played for England Schoolboys against West Germany at Wembley. By this time, dad was no longer a miner and working for British Rail, which meant free travel passes down to London.

To have my whole family watching when I played in that game was just wonderful. They were part of a crowd of 92,000 that day at Wembley Stadium. Coming out of that tunnel from the dressing rooms was quite an experience. It's something that's always stuck with me.

I don't remember much that happened on the pitch during the match, but I do remember the feeling that hit me when I walked out in front of so many people. What I do recall is that I played on the left wing and was involved in one very special moment. I was never renowned for my goal-scoring, but at 1-1 I managed to get the winner six minutes from time.

When you sign schoolboy forms at 15, you're so incredibly young and naïve and facing the prospect of living away from home and family. How big a deal was it leaving home for the first time to go to Burnley? Massive - and not just for me. My mum was with me at Todmorden station to see me off. I was upset, mum was upset, but as I travelled down on the train I thought about the exciting new challenge that awaited me in Lancashire.

CHAPTER 4
My Football League Debut

I left home that July after the World Cup in 1966 to join Burnley, who had finished third in the top division behind Liverpool [champions] and Leeds United [runners-up]. Already that year I'd played at Wembley, watched England lift the World Cup and signed for a top team. It doesn't get much better than that! All I wanted to do was be a footballer, but now the biggest challenge of all was ahead of me. I had eighteen months to prove myself. You knew that on your seventeenth birthday the manager would pull you into his office and say, "Yes, we want to offer you a professional contract" or "No, sorry we are going to have to let you go."

Was I going to make it? I know for a fact that there was only one other lad in that England Schoolboys international side I played for that went on to further his career. His name was Geoff Merrick, my captain in the England Schoolboys matches. Bristol-born, Geoff became a legend for his home-city club and played more than 350 games for them. They tell me today there's still a high failure rate from schoolboy internationals making it as professional footballers. In truth, it's probably even harder now than ever before.

Life as an apprentice at Burnley was good, but tough at times. There was a good deal of what I would now call bullying going on. None of us apprentices would go into the changing rooms to sweep up or clear up until the first-team players had gone. If you did, you got a boot thrown at you. Can you imagine that now? Thankfully, these days, the young players go into the changing rooms and listen to all the banter and stories the senior pros tell them.

As young lads do, we had our fair share of fun and played a few pranks on anyone as long as they weren't on the senior playing staff. We had a commercial manager called Jack Butterfield. He was a nice fella. As apprentices do, we had to paint the terraces at Turf Moor. One day, as we came in for some lunch after a hard morning's work, I must have come in late. You had to walk through this hall door and Jack Butterfield comes through it before me and apprentice Mick Docherty - son of Tommy Docherty - had put a bucket full of water above the door. Jack opens the door, and they all thought it was me that was supposed to get wet. It couldn't have gone better - the bucket went straight over Jack, who was drenched along with all the letters for the secretary and chairman he was carrying. Typical apprentice pranks.

Away from the football, I was well looked after in digs for six years by Walter and Winnie Edmondson at 28 Deerstone Avenue, right at the back of Burnley Football Club. When mum and dad wanted to come down and visit, they were able to stay at

Walter and Winnie's. Sharing the digs with me was team-mate Peter Jones, who will no doubt remember the regular mugs of Horlicks made with water, which I have to say was absolutely vile. Neither of us will ever forget Winnie's seemingly endless supply of Jacob's Cream Crackers and cheese. As soon as the Edmondsons had gone out, Peter and I, on the pretence of having eaten them, would throw the cream crackers out of the bedroom window like flying saucers! They were the driest cream crackers imaginable, but thankfully the meals served up at Deerstone Avenue were pretty good.

Burnley as a town was quite different back then. There were still a few smoking factory chimneys and mills in the 1960s. I'd arrived in a working-class cotton town from West Auckland, which was a pit village, so it was no great change for me. Back then, Burnley only had a population of 70,000. It was remarkable how such a relatively small community supported such an established top-level football club. Around one-third of the population would go to the matches. They had - and still do have - a massively passionate core support. The town was served by two great newspapers, the *Burnley Express* and the *Evening News*. Keith McNee was the guy I remember at the *Burnley Express*, and the *Evening News* had a reporter called Granville Shackleton. Both would make a habit of catching the Burnley first-team players at training for an interview, having approached the club first of course. Both were canny guys and very fair.

Still an apprentice, my first-team debut was at Turf Moor in May 1967 in the final match of the season. I was sub a week before that, against Arsenal, but wasn't called upon. Manager Harry Potts called me over on the Friday before the game and said, "I'm playing you against Everton."

My Burnley team-mates that day were goalkeeper Harry Thomson, Colin Blant, Les Latcham, Fred Smith, Alex Elder, John Angus, Sam Todd, Gordon Harris, Willie Morgan, Andy Lochhead and sub Brian O'Neil, who replaced big Andy during the game.

That famous Everton side had Alan Ball and Colin Harvey in midfield and Gordon West in goal, and I played against full-back Tommy Wright on the left wing. Alan Ball's father was sat next to my mum and dad in the stands. When they proudly explained, "Our son's playing today", Alan Ball senior replied, "Don't worry about your Dave - he's playing against Tommy Wright. He'll play him hard but he'll be fair." And he was right.

Even today, I'm the youngest to play for Burnley, I think. But even at sixteen I felt ready. Yes, I was pretty nervous, but I can genuinely say that I went out and thoroughly enjoyed my first game. Some people might freeze a little bit, but I was quietly confident. There's a great saying in football attributed to Dave Sexton: "When you win, lose or draw or you have a bad game you never go high, you never go low, because the funny thing about football is that you can be on the crest of a wave and all of a sudden your life can just collapse."

You can get badly injured or you can lose form, so without being full of yourself you've got to have that quiet confidence about yourself. I don't believe anyone who says they don't get nervous, but once you get out there on that pitch that feeling leaves you. You're so focused for 90 minutes - the ball comes to you, you control it and everything just comes naturally. If you feel you are having a good start - you are beating your full-back - everything clicks. Football is all about confidence. I'm a great believer in living life on an even keel. If you don't have that quiet confidence the mind can play games with you. I don't like arrogant people. I like to "never go high and never go low" as Dave Sexton said.

The result on my debut Saturday was Burnley 1 Everton 1. We took the lead, only for a certain Alan Ball to stop me starting my career with a victory, scoring the equaliser from the penalty spot. Strangely, Alan Ball, who I'd already come across when down at Blackpool for a trial when I was a schoolboy, would feature quite significantly in my future career on at least two or three occasions.

When I say I was an unused substitute against Arsenal, before my debut, that's not strictly speaking true. Subs were a new thing around that time and - until the following season - only used in place of injured players. So, I was held in reserve.

That season, with one appearance to my name, Burnley finished mid table - a league won by the fantastic Manchester United side which included Bobby Charlton, George Best and Denis Law. As a result, United qualified for the European Cup, which they'd go on to win the following season. In my debut season, Burnley weren't too shabby in the Inter-Cities Fairs Cup [the forerunner of the UEFA Cup], beating VfB Stuttgart, Lausanne-Sport and Napoli before going out to Eintracht Frankfurt in the quarter-finals. Although, of course, I hadn't been in contention to play in any of those games, I'd felt a real buzz around the club that season and most of us youth team players had tickets and attended those European home-leg games at Turf Moor.

At the start of the 1967/68 season I was still held in reserve. Burnley got off to a winning start at home to Coventry City in August and only lost four games before my second start in November at West Bromwich Albion. I remember that thrashing at the Hawthorns well. Just as well I didn't make my debut in the 8-1 defeat Burnley suffered that day. I would never have played again! One thing I can never forget about that game. Remember, in those days you could pass the ball back to the goalkeeper. Well, our goalkeeper was a Scots guy called Harry Thomson. Unfortunately, Albion opened the scoring that day when my team-mate Arthur Bellamy passed the ball back to Harry and we all turned round waiting for him to punt it up the field. Sadly, the ball went straight through Harry's legs! Tony Brown and Jeff Astle murdered us after that. It was a nightmare performance.

My next game a month later didn't go much better either. Another thrashing: this time 5-1 at Coventry City. I was being used sparingly and only reappeared in the first XI in a 1-1 draw at home to Wolves. What seemed like my once-a-month selection, this time in March, at least saw me on the winning side at last as Burnley eased past Southampton at Turf Moor, 2-0. I still didn't keep my place, though, only returning in April for the 2-0 victory at Leicester City, the 2-1 defeat to Chelsea at Stamford Bridge and the May 0-2 reverse at home to Sheffield United. Thankfully, I turned out for the final home game when Leeds United were dispatched 3-0.

While I was still not experienced enough to be a first-team Burnley regular, my other focus that season was increasingly on a wonderful run in the FA Youth Cup. Despite Burnley's pedigree as a club that encouraged and invested in youth, they had, perhaps surprisingly, never won the competition.

During the first and second rounds, at least two afternoons a week, first-team coach Jimmy Adamson took training for the youth team, working on tactics and free kicks. Not something that would happen today.

Adamson's time with the youth team was well spent as we thumped Yorkshire Amateurs 7-0 before claiming the scalps of

Manchester City, then Manchester United, Sheffield United and Everton, to secure a place in the final.

We played Coventry City in the final, and who should be in goal that night but David Icke, who would become less famous as a footballer but better known for his writing, broadcasting, public speaking and theorising. Coventry also fielded Willie Carr, Graham Paddon and Jeff Blockley, who made decent football careers for themselves. The final was over two legs and the second leg was at Turf Moor. Trailing 2-1 from the first leg, we knew what we had to do. It was a dreadfully wet, muddy night in front of around 15,000. Happily, we beat Coventry 2-0 and it was an honour to be a part of the first FA Youth Cup win in Burnley's history.

Our line-up that night speaks volumes for the youth policy Burnley Football Club believed in so strongly: Gerry McEvoy, Peter Jones, Mick Docherty, Wilf Wrigley, Eddie Cliff, Eric Probert, Alan West, David Hartley, Willie Brown, Steve Kindon, me and substitute George Coppock. Almost all of us were about to play at the highest levels professionally.

On my seventeenth birthday, I duly signed my first professional contract for Burnley. At most clubs it would have been a stressful year or so for a number of hopefuls like me. But, unusually, quite a few of us apprentices became pros around the same time - mostly due to our FA Youth Cup win that year.

Now I was earning a decent wage. Burnley paid well. I was on about £50 basic a week with a bonus on top. At times I could be getting, at seventeen, about £90, which was a lot of money in those days. I can't remember exactly what the bonuses amounted to, but if it was a goal bonus I would never have been paid!

Earning good money, once I'd bought my first car, I was back and forth to West Auckland whenever possible. It was a new Vauxhall Viva, which I saved up for along with the leather jacket that I wore in the photo all footballers seemed to pose for back then in front of their cars. According to one newspaper I was now part of "football's young elite". But I wasn't one for partying or living a lavish lifestyle. When I did go out it was often to the beautiful countryside outside Burnley, which was fantastic. That car gave me a lot of freedom.

I'd buy the latest music cassettes and super8 cartridges for the car. The Beatles were fantastic but I was probably more into my Tamla Motown, and The Moody Blues were a big favourite.

I was not a nightclub boy. That was never my scene. I was quite a home bird really, dedicated to football, and I made sure I got plenty of rest and looked after myself.

CHAPTER 5

First-Team Regular: I Get My Chance

The 1968/69 season kicked off with me in the Burnley line-up from the off. For the first time it appeared that Harry Potts was selecting me as a first-team regular. I'd played in the last game of the previous season with Scottish winger Willie Morgan, who, during the summer, was transferred by Burnley to Manchester United. Another fine Burnley winger and midfielder, Ralph Coates, was substitute that day. Now, with Morgan gone and Ralph and I more established first-team members, we began the season at the City Ground with a creditable 2-2 draw with Nottingham Forest. The Forest line-up that day was decent. We were up against Ian Storey-Moore, Jim Baxter, Henry Newton, Terry Hennessey and a striker by the name of John Barnwell, who would play a part in my career for all the wrong reasons nine years later when he was Wolves' boss.

Our one big problem that season was inconsistency. I was enjoying myself, but our form was certainly up and down. Typical

43

Burnley at the time, we'd win a couple then lose a couple. We were also capable of losing heavily. There was a late-August thumping at Upton Park with Trevor Brooking (2), Geoff Hurst (2) and Martin Peters sharing the goals in a 5-0 demolition.

In September, inspired by a Jimmy Greaves hat-trick, Spurs thrashed us 7-0 at White Hart Lane before we managed a 1-0 victory a week later at home to Manchester United.

In front of a full house of almost 33,000, this win had extra significance that season as United were European champions and competing for the Intercontinental Cup in the same month we played them. United's two-leg tie against South American champions Estudiantes de La Plata was big news that autumn. In a way, our win against United was significant for me personally, too. Returning to Turf Moor for the first time, Willie Morgan was in the United side that day, alongside Bobby Charlton, Denis Law and George Best.

Morgan had held down the position in the Burnley team line-up that I'd now made my own since his £110,000 transfer to Old Trafford. He was a good player, but I never really took to Willie when he was at Burnley. He was a bit too full of his own importance for me.

While Manchester United were undoubtedly the glamour club of that era, they did attract their fair share of hooligan supporters. The only times I remember any real trouble at Turf Moor was when United were the visitors. I'm sure they weren't the only badly behaved fans, but they travelled in such large numbers and on at least one occasion completely wrecked Burnley town centre, smashing windows on a trail of destruction. In those days, back in the '70s, fans could get at one another easily from the standing terraces. Personally, I never felt threatened or intimidated by what was going on in the crowd if there was trouble at one of our games. Perhaps surprisingly, I don't remember anyone throwing anything at me apart from a snowball that hit me on the head when I was taking a corner at Coventry! The verbal abuse I do remember though. And the racial abuse became a big problem that sadly still hasn't been completely eradicated even today.

Life as a first-team regular got even better for me in our next home match after the Manchester United victory when I scored both goals - my first for the club - in a 2-1 win against Chelsea. By October we were flying, enjoying six consecutive league victories - no mean feat in the top division of English football. Easily the most eye-catching of those wins was the 5-1 beating we handed out to Leeds United at Turf Moor in October. Don Revie's men only lost one other league fixture all season and comfortably won the league by a margin of six points, with Liverpool second. How good was that Leeds team? Well, just to prove how inconsistent we were, shortly before Christmas they thrashed us 6-1 at Elland Road.

As a player I never seemed to have much success in the cup competitions. It will be a recurring theme in this book! There are some raw memories. The League Cup in 1969 was one. Everyone remembers Swindon Town of the Third Division [now League One] beating Arsenal in the final in the Wembley mud in spring 1969. Who did they beat in the semi-final matches? Burnley. The home and away games ended 3-3 on aggregate after extra time, which meant a third and deciding match at The Hawthorns, West Brom. We were about to be dumped out of the competition until I popped up with a last-minute equaliser. But it was all to no avail as Swindon eventually triumphed 3-2 in extra time.

I got my first call-up for the England Under-23s in February 1970. At that time, Alf Ramsey was managing and coaching the full England team and the Under-23s. People would say that Alf was anti-wingers based on the fact that his so-called wingless wonders won the World Cup with a new formation. His 1966-winning squad actually included John Connelly, Ian Callaghan and Terry Paine - all fine wingers - but none of them made a huge impact that summer and none of them played in the final. Was I worried Alf would overlook me too? Well he had no problem selecting me for the Under-23 squads and he always played me on the wing.

Working with Alf was an honour. As a man he definitely had an aura about him, which had much to do with his control and organisation in winning the World Cup just four years earlier. He was famously quite posh when he spoke, and I always felt you needed to be on your best behaviour in his presence. He never swore as far as I recall, and he was no mug and wouldn't tolerate any messing around in the dressing room. You were also careful what you said to him. It was always a bit like treading on eggshells when Alf was about.

One quite famous story summed up Alf Ramsey perfectly. Soon after the World Cup final when Geoff Hurst scored his hat-trick, England played away, and when the team got back to Heathrow Airport, Geoff and a couple of others asked if they could share a cab back to the FA's HQ at Lancaster Gate in London. From there the players then dispersed to their homes. As Geoff got out of the cab, he said, "Thanks very much boss, see you for the next international." Quick as a flash, in deadpan fashion, Alf comes back with, "Oh will you Geoffrey?"

My Under-23 debut came on the 4th of March 1970 at Roker Park, Sunderland. It was memorable for all the wrong reasons.

The game was abandoned at half-time because of the snow, with us leading 3-1 against Scotland.

Apart from that match at Sunderland, those Under-23 games were special nights and drew some decent crowds around the country. Over 28,000 came along to see the thrashing of Bulgaria, 4-1 at Plymouth. That April night we played really well and there was talk that one or two of us might make the summer's World Cup squad and go to Mexico. But Alf wasn't going to gamble on us when he had what many believed was the strongest England squad ever.

As it turned out, the senior England team lost after leading 2-0 against West Germany in the World Cup quarter-final in Mexico. That made my next cap for the Under-23s in October that same year even more satisfying than usual. It came in a 3-1 victory we enjoyed over West Germany Under-23s at Leicester City's old Filbert Street ground, in front of a crowd of 25,000. The future looked bright.

As sports writer Ken Jones put it, "Sir Alf Ramsey was surely encouraged by the sight of England goals struck with fearsome power and accuracy at Leicester last night."

The goal-scorers were Royle, Robson and Kidd for England and Weiss for West Germany. It's interesting to note the starting eleven that night: Shilton (Leicester City), Edwards (Manchester United), Robson (Derby County), Todd (Sunderland), Lloyd (Liverpool), Piper (Portsmouth), Thomas (Burnley), Kember (Crystal Palace), Royle (Everton), Currie (Sheffield United) and Kidd (Manchester United).

I absolutely loved playing with some of those lads in the Under-23s. Tony Currie was one of the game's mavericks, but he had such ability. So strong and comfortable on the ball, and wonderful vision. I still see him occasionally today, and I believe he still works in hospitality at Sheffield United, where the fans idolize him. Another one of the England Under-23 boys I remember well was Frank Worthington. He had charisma. He was like the Elvis Presley of football! Winklepicker shoes, flash shirts. Frank loved the ladies. I actually found him to be quiet and unassuming at times, but he was a larger-than-life legend in the eyes of Bolton Wanderers and Leicester City fans when he played for them.

I was enjoying playing for Burnley and enjoying playing for my manager. Harry Potts was my first manager in professional football and like a father to me. Harry wasn't a great coach, but had the man-management skills required to get us performing to the best of our ability. I'd argue he was ahead of his time in some respects. He could psych people out like a lot of the top coaches do these days. He was someone I just took to. If I had a really bad game he wouldn't say "You've let me down there…"

Some managers could be quite ruthless towards you, but I never felt that with him. As a coach he was perfect for me. He just wanted me to use my natural ability. I knew what to do once I got the ball - it was instinctive. Obviously your first touch is so important. Just watch Lionel Messi and you marvel at how good he is, but it's his first touch that so often gives him the edge.

As a winger I wasn't renowned for my goal-scoring. My job was to deliver crosses from wide areas so somebody else did, usually a big, old-fashioned centre forward. My personal battle was me against the opposition full-back. Some days I'd have the better of the full-back and some games the full-back would come out on top. Form was the key word. But what is it exactly? No one knows how you come in and out of form. Up against any opponent I mostly felt confident and would take them on, but sometimes a little bit of self-doubt would creep in. The full-back might nick the ball away from you and the crowd might give you some aggro. Crowds react instantly to how you play and they might sometimes boo or yell out "Get off Thomas!" Remember, as a winger you are very close to the crowd, so you get to hear more. I was a dribbler, and I was quick over 10 or 20 yards, but it was my crossing ability that was my biggest asset.

Now that I was playing most weeks in the first team I could appreciate the great players I was up against. People always ask me which stars from the '60s and '70s impressed me most. There's only one for me really: George Best. But the funny thing is that when he played against us for Manchester United he never played well. It wasn't a secret why he struggled against Burnley. We had a north-east lad from Crook Town called Les Latcham -'Latch', as we called him - who tended to play in the Burnley reserves a lot. He was a good squad player, but every time we played Man. United Harry Potts and Jimmy Adamson would call for 'Latch'. He had that way of reading what George was going to do. And on a Monday after the game, without fail he'd come out with the same joke: "Come on George, come out of me top pocket." He had that knack of playing against him. Perfect when 'Bestie' was playing, but sometimes if you put 'Latch' against another winger he'd be hopeless!

But for me George was the best. He was unbelievable. He came on the scene at about seventeen and for the first four or five years he was brilliant. As an opposition footballer you look at the strengths and the weaknesses of an individual. With 'Bestie', he had everything. He was quick, brave, he could head a ball, scored goals, tackled. His balance was just amazing. You could never knock him off the ball. Playing on the wing, as I did, you weren't expected to be a great header of the ball. We weren't the best at tackling. George was. He had it all and gave us so many wonderful memories.

Remember that lovely TV clip of him running half the length of the pitch against Chelsea under the lights at Old Trafford? Ron 'Chopper' Harris came across and tried to whack him so hard and George's legs buckled. If that had been done today, Harris would have been sent off, but 'Bestie' rode the tackle, Chelsea keeper Peter Bonetti came out, George pretended to shoot, he went round him and rolled the ball into the net. Sensational.

Sadly, as we all know, he lost it. Apart from playing against him I only met him twice. He was a humble and very, very quiet guy. Of all places, I met George at the Butlin's Bognor Regis holiday camp. I was in his company a lot while he was down there. I used to do some coaching there. Very respectful, always acknowledged you. God's gift to football, I'd say.

Despite Alf Ramsey winning the World Cup without wingers just a few years earlier, this was still the era of some great players who hugged the touchline, took on defenders and could cross a ball. Thank goodness my grandfather forced me to use my left foot all those years ago when he coached me as a boy. In my professional football career, I was mainly the corner-taker and I'd take them with either foot. Not a problem. It was a big advantage for me. If I was on the left wing I'd mostly take them with my right foot, and on the right wing with my left. Not all the great wingers I played against were two-footed, but some of them had other ways to make an impact.

Peter Thompson was one of the best wingers I've ever seen. We played his Liverpool side at Burnley once and we'd just signed a full-back - coincidentally, Jimmy Thompson. Peter absolutely tore Jimmy to shreds. Arsenal's George Armstrong was another: great two-footed player, and also a real work horse for the Gunners. Then there was Steve Heighway. Steve joined Liverpool from non-league football and was a very wiry player with great pace and ability. Mike Summerbee from Manchester City always impressed me. He was tough. Where most wingers were normally a bit fancy - they don't tackle and jump out of the way when they get challenged - Summerbee could handle himself. Another just like Summerbee was a guy called Johnny Morrissey, who was playing for Everton the day I made my debut for Burnley. He made an impression. He'd break your leg, given half a chance! He did just that to Burnley's Willie Irvine. Morrissey was the toughest winger around back then. Southampton's Terry Paine also fell into the same category. Another of our full-backs at Burnley, my team-mate John Angus - probably one of the best full-backs I've played with - came a cropper against Paine. He went completely over the top and did John. Paine was renowned for that kind of thing.

Wingers did go in and out of fashion. But, in time, the pacey wide men seemed to be back in fashion once Tommy Docherty took over at Manchester United. I enjoyed watching Gordon Hill and Steve Coppell in what was basically a 4-2-4 formation.

If I had to vote for my all-time favourite winger, Nottingham Forest's John Robertson would come top of my list. He was probably as good as you'll ever see. He was quite dumpy for a winger. 'Cloughie' bought him and Forest had that golden patch. John had two good feet and I'm a great fan of any right-footed left winger, if that doesn't sound too daft. Robertson was in that class, whereas someone like Manchester City's Peter Barnes was good but you could always force Peter inside as his left foot was his strongest. With John Robertson, you never knew which way he was going to go. He was a great crosser of the ball too. What I liked was that he dropped his shoulder and you'd think he would pull the ball wide, but he'd still get a fantastic cross in.

As far as the teams we came up against at Burnley were concerned, Liverpool were a cut above. The Shankly era with Tommy Smith, Ron Yeats, Ian St John - they were big characters. Tottenham Hotspur were always a difficult side for us. I try to forget Jimmy Greaves tearing us apart at White Hart Lane, and they had centre-half Mike England, who was always impressive, and of course, hardest of them all, Dave Mackay. He was certainly not a player you ever felt you wanted to mix it with! Dave was softly spoken but tough as they come for Spurs and then Derby County. Frank McLintock, I always rated. He led Arsenal to the double. I was fortunate to play alongside Frank later for QPR. Those were monumental teams.

But to be fair, the opposition never really liked going to Burnley. It was always a hard game for them. Talking of hard men, we had Andy Lochhead and 'Ralphie' Coates. To get a result at Turf Moor you had to work for it. We were very well respected by other clubs. That toughness had been instilled down the years by a succession of great characters playing for Burnley. The likes of Jimmy Adamson, Jimmy McIlroy, Brian Pilkington and Ray Pointer had set the standard.

I think the FA Youth Cup win had helped bond some of the younger lads. That success and togetherness had filtered through to the first team. Burnley was always a well-drilled and disciplined football club. There wasn't much of a drinking culture when I was there, but that didn't mean to say alcohol didn't play a big part in the off-field lives of one or two of the players.

Among my team-mates was a lad called Eric Probert. Eric had actually come through the youth set-up and played and won the FA Youth Cup with me. Eric had a big problem. I would pick him up on the way to training every morning and he used to absolutely stink of alcohol. Despite this, he was hard as granite, a tough Yorkshireman - the sort of player who would get drunk but still train to a great level the next morning. Sadly, he passed away in his early fifties.

But, as I've said, we didn't have the situation where groups of players went out drinking too much, even though in those days a pint and a fag were pretty commonplace. It did get out of hand at other clubs. Later, when Alex Ferguson took over at Old Trafford, Bryan Robson, Paul McGrath and Norman Whiteside were renowned for it. 'Fergie' got rid of all that. These were great players and they managed to get away with it, up to a point. But with all the foreign players coming into our game, eventually drinking excessively became a thing of the past. The foreign players showed our lot how to look after themselves.

So, old-fashioned discipline and organisation was what Burnley was all about. That, along with some really creative ideas in the coaching, and the fantastic Gawthorpe training ground, meant that the club was years ahead of its time. The Burnley policy was to invest in young players, coach them, get them in the first team and sell one a year.

They had a wonderful chairman called Bob Lord, who was a butcher by trade and a very successful multi-millionaire businessman. He was an iconic character in Burnley's history. In the winter I always remember him wearing a beautiful long coat with a velvet collar and a bowler hat. We were playing away at Sheffield Wednesday once and I accidentally sat on that bloody bowler hat! I was sat up front on the team bus, and after I'd ruined his hat I was very polite and apologetic, but as you can imagine he wasn't happy.

Bob Lord, or Sir Bob Lord as he later became, was the heart of Burnley Football Club. When we travelled as a team we stayed in the best hotels and he made sure we were well looked after. He was quite a frightening character, very dogmatic and famously argumentative, but he worked tirelessly for the club.

I'll never forget how well he looked after us players and I'll always be grateful for that. And it wasn't just financially. Although we were always well paid at Burnley, what made the club special was the family atmosphere. My mum and dad were welcome in the boardroom and Bob Lord's wife and manager Harry Potts' wife were always about the place making everyone feel at home.

Bob Lord could be very generous. Every Christmas, each of the Burnley players was given an enormous turkey by him. The average weight of those birds was 25 lb. They were so big we couldn't get his turkey in our oven!

Traditionally, Christmas was a really busy period for us pro footballers. If we ever managed to cook one of the chairman's turkeys, all the players were given time off to eat the full Christmas dinner and all the trimmings with their families. However, at all the clubs I played for we always trained together on Christmas morning. Typically, we would be in early at 10 a.m. for a small-sided game and a check on injuries, and then we'd be showered and home by 12.30.

During my six years at Burnley, I served under two managers. When I joined the club Harry Potts was manager, but I soon realised that nothing stays the same for long in football. After years of success, his time as Burnley boss was coming to an end in 1970. Serving under Harry Potts was first-team coach Jimmy Adamson. Then Jimmy took over as boss. In an example of how much of a family club it was, the chairman moved Harry upstairs and kept him on. Harry Potts, as I've already said, had been like a father figure to me. His successor had a quite different management style.

Jimmy Adamson was born and raised in the famous footballing mining town of Ashington in Northumberland, where the Milburn and Charlton footballing families were from.

During his reign as manager at Burnley I thought he was a wonderful coach, although I didn't get on particularly well with him personality-wise. But as a coach he was second to none and I learned a lot. Our personal clashes were mostly over things like the fashion of the day for wearing your hair a little bit longer. Jimmy didn't like that. He would tell you to get your hair cut and, as I was getting older, I felt I could stand up to him on things like that. I trusted and respected him, but not in the same way I'd felt about Harry Potts. Jimmy would build you up, but he could also make you feel really small. Some managers could try to undermine you and play mind games and he was certainly one of those.

Although I had begun my career as a winger at Burnley and first caught the scouts' attention as a left winger during my England Schoolboys appearances, later on I tended to play more as a left-sided midfielder. One reason was that a very talented young Welsh winger called Leighton James was starting to break into the Burnley side. We used to chat a lot, Leighton and I. He could upset a few people being the precocious talent he was, but he was a very good player and a decent finisher too. Like me he would number Queens Park Rangers among his clubs after his time at Burnley, although we never played together again after I left Burnley.

My free time was still spent commuting back home to County Durham at weekends. I first met my wife Brenda in 1970 on one of those occasions when I'd returned home on a Saturday having played for Burnley earlier in the day. I wasn't much of a drinker, but one of my regular haunts for a post-match wind-down drink and social chat was the Fox & Hounds pub in the lovely village of Cotherstone. Brenda was standing at the bar chatting and I was immediately struck by her and decided to pluck up the courage to ask her out on a date. It was actually the following Sunday morning when we met there again, and I took her on what would become a fairly regular tour of the Teesdale countryside for a drive and a coffee. My timing when I asked her out for that first time was, I later found out, perfect. As luck would have it, she was in the process of dumping a boyfriend, so as far as Dave Thomas was concerned, free for a limited period only! Before long, Brenda Blackbell and I began seeing quite a lot of each other. Happily, I immediately hit it off with Brenda's parents too, and the inevitable wedding bells would ring out two years later in 1972.

Towards the latter stages of my career at Burnley, the team and I were not in good form. We were relegated from the top division in 1970/71 and went out of the FA Cup at the first hurdle to Second-Division Oxford United that season. We had only managed two wins in the league at that point of the season so I suppose it came as no surprise, but the heavy 3-0 defeat hurt.

"Thomas raced 50 yards clear to produce a fine shot which Kearns tipped over the bar," reported John Parsons for the *Daily Mail*, but otherwise it was one-way traffic with a powerful Oxford, captained by Ron Atkinson, deserving their victory in front of a bumper crowd of 17,010. It was not perhaps one of the cup's biggest giant-killings, but it said much about the lacklustre nature of many Burnley performances that season. While our fate was still in the balance, Bob Lord called a special meeting at the training ground. He sat us all down and offered us a reward payment at the end of the season to keep us in the top division. His thinking was that it might gee us all up. But it failed to make the necessary impression and Burnley's 24 consecutive seasons in the top flight came to an end.

Relegation was hard to take, but we only had ourselves to blame as it had taken us 15 matches to record our first win. We said goodbye to the old First Division at Molineux, where a solitary Derek Dougan goal for Wolves was enough to beat us.

With Burnley relegated I began wondering about my future. Although I was now a Second-Division footballer I was enjoying the lifestyle. Like most, even though I didn't own a house, I invested my money in cars and clothes. On my 21st birthday I splashed out on a Jaguar XJ6 and a £60 sheepskin coat. Even the *Sunday Times* were speculating on my worth, labelling me as the 'player with the Pelé touch' and valuing me at £300,000. Slowly at first, I started to explore my options and continued thinking about a move away from Burnley.

Burnley didn't exactly set Division 2 alight in the 1971/72 season and I finally reached a stage in the summer where I felt the club, and more specifically Jimmy Adamson and I, needed to part company. I had a lot of time for Jimmy, but we had one confrontation too many. I respected his new ideas as a coach, but as a person not so much. That said, maybe I wasn't the easiest of players to deal with. I'd stand up to him and disagree with him, and whether or not he liked that approach I'm not sure. He continued his way of building you up one day and then having a go at you in front of other players the next. He really did make you feel like his number-one player at times, but he'd slaughter you publicly when he thought he needed to. I absolutely detested that. If a manager went for me in front of other people I was finished with them. Half-time comments such as "You need to get your finger out" - fine. I respected that. But full-on verbal attacks in front of your team-mates? No way. No one deserves that. A coach like that was my worst nightmare in football and I wouldn't stand for it. Jimmy just didn't have the man-management skills we'd all experienced when Harry Potts was boss.

Another thing that began to bother me in the summer of 1972 was my fitness.

Although I'd always enjoyed playing in the England Under-23 games, I did suffer a good deal of pain in one tour match we played in East Germany. I collapsed in agony midway through the second half. My calf muscles were as hard as rocks. Everyone has cramp from time to time, but this was horrendous. I'd first suffered the problem when I was a kid. Maybe it was due to my lack of game time at Burnley - I was on the transfer list - but it was a cramp that wouldn't shift.

Alf Ramsey put me on a course of salt tablets, a remedy he said had worked wonders for Alan Hudson. So far from home, it was difficult to look on that tour to East Germany and Poland with much enthusiasm, particularly as half the squad were carrying assorted injuries. We literally limped into our hotel in Warsaw, as one newspaper headline put it.

Fortunately, my painful experience behind the Iron Curtain didn't last long and reports in the press that I might struggle to remain in top-class football were soon quashed. Those rumours hadn't exactly helped my chances of a move away from Burnley.

Now I was on the list, at least everyone knew I was available and there was one potential transfer that didn't go through that is still worth a mention. I nearly signed for Brian Clough.

While staying at Brenda's mum and dad's house in Sunderland, the phone rang and it was Jimmy Adamson, who said, "Derby County boss Brian Clough would like to see you."

So, of course, I drove down from the north-east on my own to meet him at the Higher Trapp Hotel in Simonstone, just outside Burnley. Burnley chairman Bob Lord was there waiting, along with Jimmy Adamson. Apparently the fee was £230,000, which would have been a British record at the time, I think. I'm absolutely bricking it sitting in the Higher Trapp with 'Cloughie' and Peter Taylor and they grilled me for ages about everything under the sun apart from the fee and my salary. To this day I've no idea why I didn't sign. 'Cloughie' shook my hand afterwards and off he went. They left me in limbo. Typical Brian Clough: with the money they were going to spend buying me, a winger, they went out and bought Leicester City's David Nish, a full-back, instead. Never spoke to him or heard from him ever again!

Apparently, Bob Lord and Jimmy Adamson were just as puzzled as I was that the deal had come to nothing.

I wasn't happy starting the new season still playing in the old Second Division. That said, Burnley made a pretty good start to the 1972/73 season and I featured in ten games. But I still wanted away.

Although I felt I was playing well, my Burnley career ended with a suspension after a rash of bookings. It wasn't a regular thing throughout my time in professional football. I only got sent off once, and as you can imagine it certainly wasn't for my tackling. I was frustrated and upset. It was at Ashton Gate, Bristol City's ground, and I told the ref to "f off!" So I went straight down the tunnel, got myself a cup of tea and waited for a bollocking from the manager. Not nice. I felt isolated and obviously I'd let the team down.

Generally, I got on alright with the refs. Let's face it they have a difficult job. And it's become a hundred times more difficult these days. Camera angles, ear pieces, VAR - I know they are professional and well paid, but they are under incredible scrutiny and pressure. VAR has got to be good. There's so much at stake. A manager can get sacked, a goal chalked off - things that are sometimes a direct result of an unsighted refereeing decision. It's all too important not to have technology helping refs. If you look at the referees and the assistant referees they don't get it wrong too often, but in this day and age the technology that brings us such great TV coverage should also be used to help them.

I'm not sure how the referees in my day would cope now. Some of them were real characters. Most memorable was Leicestershire's Roger Kirkpatrick. He was a roly-poly character, bald with massive sideburns, and looked as though he had stepped out of the pages of a book by Charles Dickens. He'd make a decision - he was always up his own backside - and then sprint quick as anything back down the pitch. Anyway, Kirkpatrick played no small part in the end of my Burnley career. Typically, he helped us out with one controversial decision but was also responsible for my ban that October. It was a game that saw Burnley keep top spot in the Division 2 table back in October 1972, when at 0-0 a shot by Colin Waldron smashed against the underside of the bar and Mr Kirkpatrick went "Goal!" Had it crossed the line? Our opponents that day, Blackpool, protested bitterly but to no avail, and we went on to narrowly beat them 4-3. It was an afternoon I'll never forget as I went on one of my long runs to score our fourth, with Blackpool defenders in pursuit before sliding the ball past John Burridge. As Peter Higgs in the *Burnley Express* observed that week, "The only disappointing news for Burnley, who remained top of the league, was a third booking in five games for Thomas, who would now serve an FA suspension. It was a blow with Thomas in outstanding form." Roger Kirkpatrick obviously had the last word that day!

I believe that was the last game I ever played for Burnley.

Having already made it clear to the club that I didn't want a move south, I waited to see what would happen. But the situation dragged on and on until out of the blue, after five months on the transfer list, there was some genuine interest in me.

At the time I read all the transfer rumours in the newspapers. If you read the *Daily Mail*, I was wanted by Everton as a replacement for Alan Ball, and Leeds boss Don Revie was quoted as saying he would be ringing Burnley to express his interest.

I don't think I was distracted. On the pitch I was still playing quite well when selected and even managed what the *Daily Express* headlined as a "wonder goal" in a 2-0 win against Preston, watched by Revie. You have to remember that in those days the clubs told their players very little when it came to the buying and selling of their assets. And you didn't get much of a say unless you stood up for yourself. So different to today's superstars, who with their agents are very much pushing for deals and moves. I knew Leeds United were interested in me but Burnley, and especially Bob Lord, hated Leeds and Don Revie so that wasn't going to happen. Having already said that I didn't want to go south, of course when the transfer did happen it was very much in that direction, but there was nothing I could do about it. Bob Lord got me in his office to tell me, "We've accepted an offer from Queens Park Rangers. The choice is yours." I could tell by the way he said it I didn't have much choice! He was arrogant that day and it was as if he was glad to see the back of me. I guess that was fair enough, because on that occasion I was glad to see the back of him!

I was leaving behind some good friends. Some of them I'm still in touch with today. My Burnley room-mates were Ralph Coates and later Paul Fletcher. While a lot of my pals had come through the youth team, Paul had been transferred in from Bolton Wanderers in a £60,000 deal. He and I became firm friends. Brian O'Neil was a character I'd miss. A good midfield player. He could be a bit aloof at times, but I remember him most as the club comedian.

Then there was Steve Kindon. Daft as a brush was 'Kindo'. He still is! Always up for a laugh. When he passed his driving test he bought a Hillman Hunter. He was always an erratic driver to say the least and he'd say things like, "I bet I can beat that car up the top of the hill to that roundabout." And he would. He'd drop a gear and off he went. He was crackers! When Brenda and I were naming a guide dog through the Name a Puppy scheme and we were searching for a name to call it we thought of Steve, and now there's a guide dog out there answering to the name of Kindo 2!

I have to be honest, the prospect of a move down to Queens Park Rangers didn't fill me with great joy. It would undoubtedly be different - but just how different?

'Different' can't begin to describe how life-changing the next few years would be, both on and off the pitch.

CHAPTER 6
Going South

A lovely man called Brian Miller, who was on the Burnley coaching staff and a football stalwart at the club, drove me to Manchester's Piccadilly Station and I caught a train south. On my arrival in London, Queens Park Rangers chief scout Derek Healey met me and whisked me off to meet Rangers boss Gordon Jago. All the way down on the train and then in the meeting, I'm thinking this is a massive step. From a little town in Lancashire to the bright lights of London would be a huge contrast.

My first impressions were good. I took an instant liking to Jago. Although he hadn't managed for long in the English game, Gordon had made quite an impact in North America's National Professional Soccer League before his appointment at Loftus Road. He'd even managed the United States national team for a short while. He was my sort of man: a caring, normal guy. So I signed for Queens Park Rangers, who, like Burnley, were in football's second tier.

As it turned out, the fee was a record for a Division 2 club. Rangers were paying £165,000 for my services.

The deal had been reported as "the smoothest business transaction I have ever been involved in", according to Gordon Jago, but it would also prompt a national press outburst from Jimmy Adamson, who wasn't happy at all. The man incurring his wrath was Don Revie. I think Jimmy felt that some of Revie's flattering comments about me had turned my head and unsettled me at Burnley, while never actually making a bid for me to take me to Leeds.

Although it was a gamble going to QPR, somehow it felt right. Something was happening down in Shepherd's Bush and I wanted to be part of it.

Then I met the players. Well blimey! Terry Venables, Gerry Francis, Stan Bowles: all streetwise people. Surprisingly, I just fitted in. My new team-mates were all brilliant to me and I felt comfortable in my new surroundings almost immediately. Things were changing fast at Rangers. Stan Bowles had only arrived a month earlier from Carlisle United, where he had been rattling in the goals.

The club were definitely on the up, and very soon I forgot my disappointment that I hadn't managed to get a move to a top-division northern club. I soon discovered that Rangers were a progressive outfit, even though they had recently lost the services of their star player, Rodney Marsh. He was, as everyone told me, the king of Loftus Road. The chairman, Jim Gregory, had clearly loved him, but he'd left Rangers to join the Manchester City side managed by Malcolm Allison. Rodney was a maverick and, from what I'd been led to believe by the players, pretty much un-coachable. Would you have wanted him in the trenches with you? Perhaps not, but he was idolized by the QPR fans and was a great talent who had averaged a goal every other game over more than 200 appearances for the club. The best description I can give you about 'Marshy' is that he was a bit like a circus act. He could juggle a football like no one else I've seen - apart from perhaps Stan Bowles. Can you imagine both of them two in the same Rangers side? Two massive egos. That wouldn't have worked. Now it was Bowles, another maverick, who had taken over Marsh's famous No. 10 shirt.

My Queens Park Rangers debut was a winning one, and it came at Loftus Road. It was a tough match. We overcame Sunderland 3-2, and if Graham Barker's *Sunday Mirror* match report is to be believed, the crowd that day - 17,356 - was 6,000 above the average. "Come to celebrate the arrival of Thomas" the paper reckoned. Well I don't know about that.

I began okay, but didn't do much of note. In some of the early games at QPR I was selected on the left side of midfield, replacing a lad called Martyn Busby, who had recently broken his leg. In Martyn's position I was struggling a bit to start with. My midfield team-mate Terry Venables, who was so tactically aware when he was a player, went to talk to Gordon Jago and coach Bobby Campbell. Venables had such a presence and they listened to him when he said, "Have you thought about playing Dave Thomas on the wing?" That idea changed my career. Best thing that could have happened.

I had only been a QPR player for a couple of months when the date for the wedding day Brenda and I had planned came around. Life was pretty hectic. The church wedding in Romaldkirk, County Durham, was scheduled for Monday the 18th of December, which meant a good deal of driving up from the south-east and back down again. I'd been given a little time off by the club to go home and enjoy the shortest of honeymoons, but obviously I had to report back for training in time for QPR's trip to the Goldstone Ground to play Brighton & Hove Albion on the following Saturday.

The St. Romald's church service was wonderful and the reception at the nearby Morritt Hotel in Greta Bridge found me in an emotional state that rendered me speechless. I literally stood up to speak and sat straight back down again. Happy as I was, I couldn't utter a word at the appropriate moments when surrounded by bridesmaids, friends and family. I should mention that one of the wedding guests that day was my good friend and Sunderland FC captain Bobby Kerr, along with his wife Cathy. Four or five months later Bobby would go on to lift the FA Cup at Wembley as his team, managed by the legendary Bob Stokoe, beat Don Revie's mighty Leeds United in one of the most dramatic finals of all time.

My best man, Roy Long, was superb and made up for my lack of words at the reception. Roy and I had been good friends as far back as our secondary school days. Funnily enough, Roy was never interested in football at all, but we always got on very well. We lost touch for many years, but when I moved back to the north-east Roy and I got together again and now we see each other socially quite a bit. He was in the prison service before his retirement and introduced me to a good few of his friends when I returned to County Durham. So nowadays I socialise quite a lot with ex-prison wardens, including my good friends Mick Daniels and Stuart Laurie. Unlike Roy they were, and still are, keen football supporters who follow Middlesbrough and Spurs, respectively.

Anyway, surrounded by my friends and family on my wedding day, my overwhelming feeling was one of pride and joy.

The Morritt - still one of my favourite places today - did us proud with a wonderful spread, but not everything after the reception went perfectly and according to plan.

The wedding day weather was horrendous. I have never witnessed fog like it before or since. As my wife and I left County Durham to drive back down to London, for what I'm sure Brenda thought might be some swanky overnight hotel, the fog eventually made driving impossible. By the time we were well into Yorkshire, in the murk, we pulled over and spotted a potential bed for the night in the less-than-swanky Selby Fork Motel. Not quite the honeymoon Brenda had anticipated. When the fog had cleared a little the following morning, we realised our location was not much more than an overnight lorry drivers' truck stop!

After the briefest of honeymoons I returned to my QPR team-mates and began my new life as a married man. My first game back we beat Brighton away, 2-1, and our form continued to improve that winter. Our home form was particularly impressive. When my former club, Burnley, came to Loftus Road on Boxing Day we won 2-0 and won every single home game after that until the end of the season. It's worth recording that we managed a run of eleven consecutive home wins, scoring 32 goals while conceding only two.

My wing play was contributing to the team and, having settled in well, I began finding some good form. I had a lot to thank Terry Venables for. A special guy and a very knowledgeable one, he had the knack of attracting people around him and he was always smiling. After training, a lot of players would shower, get dressed and be gone out the door as quickly as possible. At QPR we'd have a cup of tea, with all the lads around Terry, and he'd always talk through the game we'd played on the Saturday. "Where do you think we went wrong?" he'd say and he'd encourage us to all join in. He was always busy while I was with him at QPR. Away from playing football with us he wrote books, co-created the hit TV series *Hazell* and loved singing. What a character.

Largely thanks to Terry my form had improved and, amazingly, by the end of that 1972/73 season we were promoted to the top division. Things couldn't have worked out much better. The run-in was impressive. It had all come full circle for me. My first game earlier in the season had been a victory over Sunderland, and we ended the season beating them at Roker Park, 3-0.

Strangely, the only team standing between us and the Second Division trophy was the club I had started the season with. Burnley finished one solitary point above us as champions.

The season hadn't quite finished, and the week before our final league game, away to Sunderland, Brenda and I were fortunate enough to be given tickets for the 1973 FA Cup final at Wembley. Sunderland beat Leeds United 1-0 that day in one of the most extraordinary finals in living memory. Brenda's mum and dad were big Sunderland fans. Brenda used to go to Roker Park with her father, who was very friendly with a guy called Jack Ditchburn. Jack's father was the millionaire chairman of Sunderland. Happily, we got to go to the final and witness Sunderland's biggest day ever: they were massive underdogs being a Second Division [now Championship] side at the time. Brenda's other connection that day was that she had been bridesmaid at Bobby Kerr's wedding and Bobby was captain of Sunderland and lifted the cup at

Wembley. Bobby and his wife had, of course, recently attended our wedding. It was an amazing day. Sunderland's victory over a really established Leeds team was a colossal thing for our region in the north-east. Leeds were the crème de la crème in those days. Sunderland manager Bob Stokoe became a household name almost overnight, and I believe a quarter of a million people turned out to see the team parade the cup through the streets shortly after the final.

Leaving Wembley after the game, we dropped Brenda's mum and dad off at the victorious Sunderland team's reception at one of the hotels in London before heading home to Wokingham, where we were now living.

Coincidentally, I got to see the FA Cup at close quarters again after that Wembley final. By chance, my QPR team were playing their last game of the season against Sunderland, who were also playing their final home game at Roker Park. In the run-in I think Sunderland had had maybe a couple of outstanding league games, because of their cup run, and at one point it looked as though they might even catch us in the promotion race. Anyway, they drew away at Cardiff only two days after the Wembley final before their last fixture of the season, against us. Incredibly, it was on the Wednesday of that same week. Talk about a fixture pile-up! Unusually, as it was the end of the season, Brenda and I drove up from London for the game. I'd asked manager Gordon Jago, "Would you mind if I drive up early, separately from the team?" and Gordon - who was a lovely guy — said, "Just make sure you get to the ground on time!"

Well, I'm not kidding, I've never seen so many people in all my life! Sunderland's cup win had certainly boosted the crowd that evening. Imagine getting over the Wear Bridge with all those people.

I remember my panic as I turned to Brenda's uncle Bob in the back of the car and said, "I'm not going to get there on time in this traffic."

So I got out and legged it as fast I could to the ground. Thankfully, somehow, I made it in time.

Maybe I was unusually pumped up but, as the game started, I scored the first goal. You could have heard a pin drop. But the game was to be a secondary drama to what went on off the pitch. Sunderland officials had thought it a good idea to place the FA Cup trophy on a pedestal on the halfway line, between both managers, Bob Stokoe and Gordon Jago. On the pitch, Rangers striker Stan Bowles, in typical fashion, said to me, "That cup's not going to be there by the end of the game."

He'd obviously planned what happened next. The ball goes out of play. Stan walks over, picks the ball up and volleys it at the FA Cup and knocks it off the pedestal, lid and everything. Wallop! Then Stan runs up the tunnel with the game going on. Next thing I remember is Bob Stokoe giving chase as Stan races inside and locks himself in the away changing room. He knew Stokoe was a fiery character. There was hell to pay. Unbelievable! Only Stan could do a thing like that. The crowd were not happy and the ref had to take all us players off. Then it all settled down and, to be fair, 'Bowlesy' came back out quickly. We actually ran out 3-0 winners, but I think it was a good time to play them as Sunderland must have been knackered and had no doubt consumed a fair amount of alcohol that week after the Wembley celebrations. They might have lost heavily to us that night, but the 1973 cup-winning team are treated like gods these days by all Sunderland supporters.

In contrast to what Sunderland achieved, the FA Cup was never very good to me as a player. QPR had enjoyed a great season in the league, but it's funny how you remember the bad days. We played Barnet, who were non-league at the time, in the Third Round. Embarrassingly they held us 0-0 at Loftus Road, although we did beat them 3-0 at their place a few days later in the replay and finally went out to Derby, beaten 4-2 in the Fifth Round.

Most close seasons I'd either go on holiday with a couple of team-mates to Spain or head back to the north-east. This one was slightly different as it was my first as a married man. I'd always kept myself pretty fit by running and keeping busy in the garden. Pre-season training would start round about the middle of July and there was a lot of hard work to be put in ahead of the first league games in mid-August. Right from when I was at Burnley I remember that those summers used to get progressively hotter - or was it just my imagination? The first day back was invariably a scorcher, which wasn't great for the early strenuous endurance tests.

That summer I had time to reflect on my move south and look forward to the prospect of playing again in English football's top league.

CHAPTER 7
Back in the Top Flight

Generally, people say that northerners are more friendly than southerners. Our experiences living around the country, as far as Brenda and I are concerned, tell us it is not at all true. Family life and our first garden helped us fit in quickly and everyone was very helpful. Leaving an industrial northern market town like Burnley to move south to QPR in London was a big cultural change, no question. Shepherd's Bush and the surrounding area totally confused me. Gerry Francis was very good to me when I first arrived. He'd pick me up from where he lived near the Chiswick flyover - a real helter-skelter place - and drive me around the area and to training. My QPR team-mates were, in a nice way, very streetwise. Terry Venables, in particular, knew a lot of people. Terry was an east-end boy, brought up in a tough, difficult area and he was a survivor. The southern lads at QPR knew how things operated. It was a million miles away from day-to-day life back in the small communities I was used to in Lancashire and County Durham. I was just 22 when I'd first arrived at QPR and not streetwise at all.

By the start of my first full season at Rangers, Brenda and I were well settled to the west of London in Wokingham, Berkshire, where we had purchased our first house together in Walter Road. We had wonderful neighbours and got to know the area. Wokingham was where we started our family, and because of that I recall those first seasons at QPR with great fondness. Thankfully, unlike a lot of footballers' wives, Brenda adapted really well too, which was a great help to me. My home life was changing, as young parents will know well, and at that football club I grew up fast. I was happy on and off the field.

As I've said, my day-to-day life as a footballer was so very different from what I was used to up at Burnley.

Training was a good example. QPR had the reputation of being a progressive club, but the facilities at the Ruislip training ground were awful. The buildings were temporary - portacabins and that sort of thing. We'd roll up for morning training and occasionally this dodgy-looking guy would arrive in the car park with a boot full of knocked-off gear. When we'd changed and were leaving, 'Harry the Coat', as they nicknamed him, would open his big overcoat, which had specially made pockets inside the full length of it. I wouldn't touch any of what he was offering, but 'Bowlesy' and 'Shanksy' and other lads would have a look at the Christian Dior ties and crocodile-skin belts and buy the stuff from him to probably flog it on and make a profit themselves. Nothing like that would ever have happened at Burnley Football Club. Unfortunately for 'Harry the Coat', he got caught and ended up serving time.

The players' lounge at Loftus Road was the centre of social activity for most of the QPR players, but it wasn't my scene. I never went inside. Not once. My routine was different. After a home game at Loftus Road I didn't hang around. Brenda and her friend Maureen would wait for me outside. Maureen Ramayon was a mad keen Rangers supporter, who together with her husband Sav, who was the QPR Ladies team manager, became very good friends with us. My post-match ritual started with a pint of ice-cold milk as soon as I entered the dressing room. Then I'd shower and change and run out of the ground as quick as I could to meet up with Brenda and Maureen. Then on our way home we'd always head for the Excelsior Hotel at Heathrow for a buffet supper.

There were a lot of hangers-on at QPR. The players' lounge became the big focal point. There was a lot of ducking and diving, and anyone could get in if they slipped the doorman a few quid. With a family at home I wasn't out and about like some of the lads, but I really loved being around them and joining in the banter. I grew up quickly in London.

There are a lot of reasons why Brenda and I remember our Wokingham home with affection. Both our daughters were born down south, and what really sticks in my memory is how both births involved me struggling to make the event due to car problems. At the time I'd just purchased a brand new Triumph Dolomite, which I bought during a trip up to Sunderland. I'd been back and forth to training in it a few times but didn't use it that much as a few of us Berkshire-based players would share the driving to Ruislip. One week it would be Don Givens, the next Ian Gillard, sometimes Phil Parkes. I was training at QPR in Ruislip one day in 1974 when our coach Frank Sibley came over and said, "Dave, I've had a call and I think your wife is going into labour."

That day I'd driven the lads up to Ruislip in my new car. Immediately after hearing what Frank had told me, I hurriedly got changed, ran out to the car park and jumped in the Dolomite. Despite it being a new car, there had been problems with the Dolomite's accelerator cable sticking. Well, on that day the bloody thing was awful. I thought I was going to die! We had to get on the A40 through Slough and it was a good 50-minute drive back to Wokingham. The flaming accelerator kept sticking and I thought we were going to crash because when we'd come to a roundabout we were at about three- or four-thousand revs. But all I wanted to do was get to Wokingham Hospital maternity unit as soon as I could. To say it was quite a daunting journey would be an understatement. Thankfully I just made it in time to see Helen born and all was well.

Incredibly, history just about repeated itself two years later for the birth of our second daughter. In February 1976, Polly was born in the early hours of the morning and, typical me, I had no fuel in the car! I was so well prepared in every way this time apart from the lack of fuel. This time we had visions of pushing the Dolomite as Brenda and I kept our eye on the petrol gauge needle. Fortunately, it was only a five- or ten-minute drive to the maternity unit this time so, although it was an anxious journey, it was at least a short one.

Again, as with Helen, Polly arrived without a problem. And I wouldn't have missed being present at those births for anything. Brenda always says, given the chance, I would like to have delivered both of them - I was very hands on. I was in my element. Neither birth fazed me at all. In fact, I've often thought how much I would love to have been a doctor. The medical profession always fascinated me.

As a footballer dad, it enabled me to see more of the girls

growing up. Us London-based players would train from eleven o'clock to allow time for the traffic to ease. Then we'd finish about one o'clock and be home by two or three. All my afternoons were spent at home with the family. I was very fortunate. A lot of parents don't get that opportunity to see their children grow up like that.

I've always been very close to my girls. These days Helen is one of the deputy head teachers at Epsom College in Surrey and Polly is an events manager at Sheffield University. Both are married with two lovely boys each. Tom and Teddy are down south and James and Oliver are up north. Polly rang me the other day to say that James had been off school with a cold and was watching me from the settee play for QPR on YouTube on their new smart TV, which was nice.

If I had some time to myself away from football, whenever possible I'd spend it in the garden at home. I bought myself a plastic greenhouse, but very shortly afterwards regretted buying that. I decided I wanted a glass one and set about erecting it on the back of our garage. I may not be the best at DIY, but I am the best at reeling in contacts to help me! My gardening friend and neighbour John Tye would set to work while I was playing football on a Saturday and week by week that greenhouse grew and grew.

When I wasn't gardening I'd take myself for fishing lessons. I'd always been interested, but when I moved to Wokingham it all kicked off properly for me when I began my love of fly fishing. Just 15 minutes away was a place called Black Swan Lake and, as happens with a hobby like fishing, the more I went the better I got. None of the other players were into fishing or gardening. I think I was a bit of a nerd to them really. Planting plants and digging weren't things we discussed at training, although there was always a quip or two, such as "How are your tomatoes doing Dave?!"

My reputation as the gardening footballer began to spread as various newspapers ran features - most of them with photos - with headlines about my 'green fingers'. All good fun, but I have to say I was really passionate about that garden in Wokingham. So much so that when I was away from home I'd ring up Brenda if there was a frost forecast and ask her to light the paraffin heater to make sure my tender plants survived. It was a running joke that I'd always ask about my precious plants before asking how she and the children were! Yes, I was different all right. You can't imagine Sergio Agüero digging his vegetable patch these days, can you?

If my lawn at home at Wokingham was my pride and joy, you couldn't say the same about the playing surface at Loftus Road.

I was reminiscing with my old QPR team-mate Ian Gillard recently about how bad it got at times, and he reminded me that on one occasion the chairman even hired a helicopter to hover over the pitch to dry it out. As a stadium, Loftus Road wasn't the biggest and was quite compact and enclosed. The mud and standing water made it atrocious. Our groundsman Alex had one hell of a job. The poor man - lovely, caring guy he was - sadly had a nervous breakdown, but the state of the ground was one of the worst I played on. Like a mud heap it was at times. The pressure just got to Alex in a really bad way. He was on a hiding to nothing. Worse still was Derby County's Baseball Ground. Absolutely awful that was. But rain, snow, mud - we had to deal with all of that, but it never bothered me too much. In fact, I took quite an interest in the subject of grass, being a fanatical gardener! When out on the pitch, or at home on my lawn, I would always religiously replace divots. I would chat to Alex and all the other groundsmen at the clubs I played for. "Good light and good ventilation," I remember Alex telling me, "if you want a good playing surface." I don't think Loftus Road had much of either of those requirements, where as up the road at Arsenal the groundsman at Highbury seemed to win the award for the best kept pitch every year. Highbury was bigger, more open and got plenty of sun. It was a wonderful playing surface: just like the QPR pitch is today. Amazing what technology can do. It's like a bowling green these days.

So, perhaps the biggest difference from the '70s and '80s to the modern game today are the conditions of those pitches back then.

Apart from the time when an England Under-23 game I was playing in was abandoned at half-time because of the snow, I can't remember too many times when the weather beat us. Usually, as long as the surface was flat and not rutted, we'd play. Mind you, there was occasionally some skulduggery when it came to matches going ahead or not. One time when QPR were playing Leeds United at Elland Road, and maybe Leeds had four or five players injured and unavailable for selection, there was some really bad weather that necessitated a pitch inspection. It was a really frosty weekend. We were having a good run and Leeds were having a few injuries. As much as I liked Don Revie - he was always alright with me - he was renowned in the game for getting at referees and saying the pitch wasn't playable if it suited him. Revie, without doubt, would have been down at Elland Road telling the referee, "You've got to get this off."

On this occasion our coach, Steve Burtenshaw, and Gordon Jago went down to the ground early at the same time and the game went ahead. That was mostly Steve's influence. The pitch that day was really flat but rock hard. In those days, people like Revie would think nothing of watering the pitch and letting it ice over, but Steve was quite streetwise, whereas Gordon would have just stayed in the hotel and waited for the phone call to come.

Down south the pitches were better. As I've already said, Arsenal's old Highbury playing surface was the best, but I also rated the pitches at Ipswich Town and Leyton Orient, which were always good. Not that I played there much, but up north Carlisle United had the most unbelievable surface. All the turf for Wembley years ago used to come from Carlisle.

It was very satisfying to be back in the top league again with QPR, although I can't say we started the 1973/74 season particularly well. We had to be patient and wait six league games for our first win, which came in a five-goal thriller at West Ham United.

It was a game I'll never forget. I mostly managed to avoid the really bad, dangerous tackles. The exception was that game at Upton Park, which involved an incident that left a permanent dent in my leg. Straight from the kick-off, a ball was laid back to our midfielder Don Masson and we had a ploy where I would get on my bike and get down the wing to take Don's pass. Frank Lampard senior had obviously set his stall out, as they say, that night. Then wallop! I never saw Frank coming and he put a hole in my leg that I've still got to this day. He lunged at me and the result wasn't pretty.

I was carried off without any hope of returning. Lampard wasn't sent off, which didn't go down particularly well with my team-mates. Frank McLintock and Dave Webb would have killed him if they'd got hold of him, but they were held back. Lampard cleaned me out that night, but there was some consolation as we won the game 3-2.

That kind of foul wasn't unusual, and there was always trepidation about certain players who were renowned for kicking their opponents. It was sometimes more psychological than physical. You knew some full-backs had a reputation for whacking you, but generally speaking most were hard but fair. Paul Reaney at Leeds always liked to give me a kick and Liverpool's Tommy Smith would dish it out, but I think one of the hardest full-backs I played against was a guy called John Gidman. He played for Aston Villa and then moved to Manchester United. He was fair and quick, which was a combination that I found difficult. As far as unsettling opponents goes, Johnny Giles was a master at that. Nice chap, 'Gilesy', off the pitch - I had a lot of time for him - but for a little guy he could really handle himself. Vicious at times. Terry Paine was another, but surprisingly, hard men like Norman Hunter and Billy Bremner at Leeds I always found to be tenacious but fair. Obviously, I should mention Ron 'Chopper' Harris! If he hit you or caught you, you'd never get up. He was a tough guy. Players did seek out opponents with premeditated fouls in those days and feuds were common. Retribution wasn't always dished out by the player who'd been 'done'. It might be one of your team-mates who'd do the job for you. If someone had seriously hurt and injured your team-mate, you might not respond with retribution the next game, you might wait a year. Some players had long memories and Jack Charlton, I think, blacklisted certain players. Another prime example was Roy Keane. Everyone remembers the incident involving Alf-Inge Håland, who was playing for Leeds against Keane at Elland Road in 1997 when the Irishman injured his anterior cruciate ligament trying to tackle the Norwegian. Håland went over to the injured Keane and suggested he get up as he was feigning injury. This didn't go down well with Keane, who was stretchered off and Håland was merely booked. Keane blacklisted Håland but didn't 'do' him until more than three years later. The resulting foul on Håland's leg was a serious, career-threatening challenge, and knowing a red card would follow he didn't hesitate. Keane removed his captain's armband and walked towards the tunnel before the ref had reached for his pocket.

Anyway, QPR got off the mark with that win at West Ham without me, and other satisfying results included a 2-2 draw at high-flying Leeds United (when I managed to get on the score sheet) and exactly a month later on New Year's Day, when Tommy Docherty's Manchester United visited Loftus Road.

We were on the up and United were on the way down. They were already struggling before they came to Loftus Road, but we made things a whole lot worse for them by handing out a 3-0 beating, which could have been much worse if Alex Stepney hadn't pulled off a string of fine saves. A Bank Holiday crowd of 32,339 had squeezed into Loftus Road to see a Queens Park Rangers side brimming with individual flair players, now also gelling as a team, who worked really hard for one another. Don Givens opened the scoring, then Stan Bowles added two more - the second of which was one special goal. Leaving United's defenders in his wake, 'Bowlesy' weaved past at least four red shirts before dispatching the ball under the diving Stepney. It's worth recording our line-up that day, because that eleven was pretty much the side we put out most weeks at the time: Phil Parkes in goal, with Dave Clement, Terry Mancini, Frank McLintock and Ian Gillard at the back. In midfield were Terry Venables, Mick Leach and Gerry Francis, with Stan Bowles, Don

Givens and yours truly in attack. As it turned out, the Manchester United home game proved significant for one of the United line-up. Although we didn't know it at the time, it was George Best's last game for United. Sad to say, I don't remember much about his performance that New Year's Day, which says a lot really. Let's just say it was disappointing and not the Best I remember from so many other games, where you just marvelled at his ability. He was, and will always be, my all-time favourite player.

United were relegated at the end of the season, with Leeds United finishing as champions. Rangers finished a creditable eighth in that league table and we enjoyed a decent enough FA Cup run before going out in the quarter-finals to Leicester City. In the Fifth Round I'd finally managed to score my first-ever FA Cup goal in a 3-2 replay against Coventry City.

We didn't exactly set the world alight in our final six winless league games, but it was still a bit like unchartered territory for QPR. To be in the top half of the top division was an achievement and we finished as London's top club, looking down on Arsenal, Spurs, Chelsea and West Ham.

Sir Alf Ramsey was sacked as England manager in May 1974. Joe Mercer came in as caretaker manager, supervising a couple of home international matches and some friendlies before the powers that be appointed Don Revie for the Nations Cup qualifiers later that year.

Like Alf, Joe was in charge of the England Under-23 games and was manager for just about the scariest experience of my life. We'd just played a washout of a game against Turkey in Ankara on the 11th of May. With the score still 0-0, the game was abandoned at half-time due to the waterlogged pitch. We were flying back, and during the flight the plane descended very rapidly. Whether it got struck by lightning I'm not quite sure, but when you go down from such a great height, plummeting at speed, it's pretty frightening I can assure you.

A few weeks later my England Under-23 career came to an end with a 2-2 draw in France. Manager Ken Furphy's selection that day was significant for two reasons. My old Burnley mate, centre forward Paul Fletcher, had his nose broken and Paul was replaced at half-time by Bob Latchford, another No.9 who would feature greatly in my career.

CHAPTER 8

Why I Never Wore Shin Pads

There is one question that always comes up when anyone meets me for the first time. "Why did you always play with your socks rolled down and without shin pads?"

I wasn't trying to be different or difficult. I just felt I played with a greater freedom that way. Also, unusually, whatever the weather I always wore rubbers - moulded studs. People used to think I was crackers. But I think Jimmy Greaves was another who played in moulded studs and he didn't do too badly, did he?

The fact that I didn't wear proper studs didn't bother any of the managers and coaches I played for - apart from John Barnwell and Richie Barker at Wolves. Alf Ramsey and Don Revie, when I was playing for England, never mentioned it - it was just what I felt comfortable in. The right boots were essential.

When I was at Burnley, we were allowed to take a slip to the local sports shop to buy a pair of boots if you wanted something a bit more expensive than your average pair. The club would pay the standard amount and you had to pay the extra if you wanted something special. The big new name in boots when I was an apprentice was the Adidas 2000. They were made from the most wonderful soft leather and very popular with us players. So, off we'd go to Bray's sports shop in Nelson, just outside of Burnley, where we'd meet Jack Bray, a wonderful, shrewd old character who had played for Man. City and England. We used to spend the afternoon checking out all the new gear. Jack's favourite saying was, "If you pick something up in the shop, make sure you put it back where it's come from!" He was fussy like that.

At QPR my boots were Gola. There were about four or five of us - Don Givens, Stan Bowles, Gerry Francis, Frank McLintock and me - all sponsored by Gola and we'd get about one-hundred quid for the season plus free boots. The Gola representative was a guy called Andre Ward and he'd come to the training ground. 'Bowlesy', when he got in the England team, had the Adidas man visit him as well. The Adidas guy would turn up, and if you were with Gola he'd blacken out the markings and paint three white Adidas-style stripes over the boot! 'Bowlesy' had the right idea: he'd have a Gola boot on one foot and Adidas on the other, so he got double the money.

The other common question people ask me is the main differences between footballers when I was playing and footballers today. The game is obviously so much faster these days and the players so much quicker, but the organisation that goes on behind the scenes for them is unreal now. Take the footballer's diet for a start.

Food-wise, everything is carefully chosen and cooked these days. The science of what to eat and drink and when was only just beginning to come in back in the '70s. I always knew what

I was going to get at half-time - a cup of tea and a bollocking! At Burnley it was very common on some away trips to stop off. When we'd play Birmingham City or Aston Villa we'd have a pre-match meal at a place called Stone, near Stoke. That meal was sirloin steak or chicken. Apparently Leeds United would have a fry-up back then on a Saturday morning before the game at about 10.30. I remember Burnley copying that idea and I'm not sure that worked for me. Those away-day match meals we had down south were nearly always at Baileys or the Great Western Hotel at Paddington.

Then, for pre-match meals at QPR we'd go to Whites Hotel in Bayswater Road. That was our meeting point. This was around the time when players' diets began to change when Dave Sexton became manager. It's funny how I still remember those QPR match-day meals. You could have chicken, fish or baked beans. I'd always go for the fish, followed by the only choice of dessert - peaches in syrup for the sugar content. Then you finished up with coffee and honey.

This was also the era when the media and commercial opportunities were beginning to impact on the game. In a strange sort of way, it was quite rewarding to read about yourself in *Shoot!* or *Charlie Buchan's Football Monthly*. Footballers were a bit like pop stars. Magazines would ring up for an interview and ask you about where you live, what car you drive, even your favourite holiday destination, meal and colour. My mum and dad kept all those old magazines and I had a rummage through them recently when researching this book. One illustrated *Shoot!* interview tells me now that my favourite country was Norway, my weight was 11 st 8 lb, favourite food steak and my top dislike was people who aren't punctual. Nothing much has changed!

TV coverage began to broaden the game's appeal, too. The BBC's *Match of the Day* now had some serious competition. Down south it was *The Big Match* on a Sunday afternoon with Brian Moore and Jimmy Hill hosting and a panel of pundits: Derek Dougan, Malcolm Allison and 'Cloughie'. It was a formula that worked, and that was the start of it all in the '70s. The TV coverage just got bigger and bigger, and despite the fact that England hadn't qualified for the World Cup, that summer's tournament was still a big draw.

Interviews I did back then were done almost unplanned as you came out of the changing room. Now it's more planned, less spur-of-the-moment, which I think is no bad thing. Caught on the hop it was easy to maybe say something you shouldn't have. Players today are all trained and coached what to say, and what not to say.

In the 1974 close season I got a call from BBC commentator John Motson, who told me he wanted to include me in a feature he was writing for the *Radio Times*. I suppose it was prompted by Don Revie's appointment as the new England manager, and I was one of a number of young players looking to break into the full England squad. That feature, "England Expects", certainly raised my profile. Motson had asked me who my footballing hero was and I chose Tom Finney as I thought he was a good role model. Brenda accompanied me to London for a photo shoot, which resulted in me appearing on the cover of the *Radio Times* alongside Tom.

My interview with John Motson included the pretty standard question about my ambitions for the future. My reply wasn't what he expected and I explained that I hadn't particularly got any ambitions on the football field, before mentioning one quite different ambition I wanted to fulfil. "What's that?" he asked, and I said, "I want to meet my hero."

He probably thought I was about to respond with Muhammad Ali or somebody.

"He's on BBC2 - you might know him," I replied.

"Who on earth do you mean?" he continued.

Imagine his surprise when I said, "Geoffrey Smith, the gardener on *Gardeners' World*."

Well, John looked at me and couldn't quite believe what he was hearing. But bless him - he went away and organised an introduction through the BBC and soon after Geoffrey Smith rang me up.

I couldn't believe it. There was my hero, on the phone, asking me, "How far away are you from Kettlesing near Harrogate?" Blow me, he gave me his number and rang back a day later, saying, "I want you to visit me." Well, of course, I was in heaven.

I went to Geoffrey's house on the moors, which was remote to say the least. And he didn't disappoint. Seriously - he was the most inspirational man I have ever met. Exactly as he appeared on *Gardeners' World*.

After we'd been round his garden admiring his alpines, his wife made us afternoon tea and the two of them sat chatting to me and made me feel like a king.

Coincidentally, I found out that Geoffrey's favourite place in the world was Teesdale and that he was born close to where I'd grown up as a lad in County Durham. His father, it turned out, gardened at the same estate where Brenda and I had held our wedding reception.

Although I still watch *Gardeners' World* today and I enjoy watching Monty Don, who does a fine job, Geoffrey Smith will always be my hero.

The 1974/75 season got off to another shaky start. Gordon Jago resigned at the end of September and chairman Jim Gregory accepted his resignation. They had a great working relationship to begin with, but I've since heard that their respect for each other deteriorated badly during the previous close season. They fell out on a number of issues, not least the fact that Gordon had been invited to coach the England Under-23s that summer and Jim Gregory had said 'no'.

Gordon did oversee one significant QPR win though before he departed. We beat reigning champions Leeds United in what was Brian Clough's first home league game in charge at Elland Road. That was QPR's only win from the first 10 league games. Gordon's assistant, Stan Anderson, was put in charge but wasn't to last long. Stan was a quiet, genuine guy. He'd had an excellent playing career in the north-east with Newcastle United, Sunderland and Middlesbrough. I liked him but he wasn't exactly the most inspirational of coaches. A bit dour and lacking the personality needed in that QPR dressing room. 'Bowlesy' used to call him Hans Christian Andersen, as 'Bowlesy' would.

I was disappointed to see Gordon Jago depart. He'd built an attractive football team from the money the club had banked from the Rodney Marsh transfer and I'd always liked the way he handled an unusual bunch of characters. He and Steve Burtenshaw had managed Stan Bowles superbly and it was difficult to see how a new manager with new ways of dealing with Stan's wayward behaviour would succeed. One new idea that Gordon had imposed on us that had backfired had been the appointment - very short appointment as it turned out - of Jack Mansell, who came into the club. Jack had come over from Greece to coach us and sat us all down for a meeting before a game and called us a load of southern softies, which didn't go down well with the likes of Frank McLintock and Dave Webb in particular. To say he'd got off on the wrong foot would be an understatement! He was a hopeless coach. I'll never ever forget Stan Bowles, who was of course very close to Jim Gregory, walking in late as usual. Before he came and sat next to me he turned to Mansell and casually said, "You still here Jack?" Then he picked up his kit and began changing. Mansell, who had only been at the club two weeks, didn't know what to say, but after the game he got the call-up into the chairman's office and was sacked. 'Bowlesy' had obviously been tipped off by Jim Gregory and knew all day that Jack was history, which shows how close those two were. It was a strange kind of player power, but 'Bowlesy' was 'Bowlesy' and he got away with murder under Gordon Jago. The Mansells and Andersons of the football world couldn't tame him, so whoever was supposedly in control of the team next would have to cut 'Bowlesy' the right amount of slack. As it turned out, the next QPR manager would be a perfect fit for all of us - including 'Bowlesy'.

CHAPTER 9

"Sub Thomas Torpedoes Czechs"

Our points total was a worry, and by the time we ran out at home to Ipswich Town in October 1974 we had our third boss of the season. Dave Sexton took over at Loftus Road having been sacked by his former club Chelsea a few weeks earlier. Capturing Dave Sexton as QPR manager would prove to be an inspired appointment. October was an eventful month for me. I had a new coach, and rumours were circulating that I might get a call-up to the full England squad.

How do you find out you've been selected to play for England? In my case I got a phone call at home in Wokingham, just before I was about to go to training at Ruislip. It was a *Daily Mirror* reporter. "Congratulations," he said, "you've been picked for the new England squad."

There were rumours about one or two of us at QPR who might get the call. At the time we were all playing out of our skins. As it turned out, Phil Parkes, Ian Gillard, Stan Bowles, Gerry Francis and me all got called up. Of course, it was a massive thing to us. It was the pinnacle of my career. Queens Park Rangers could also feel justifiably proud that they had five players selected.

Don Revie had just been appointed England's new manager. He'd said some complementary things about me in his newspaper column when he was Leeds' boss that encouraged me to think I might be involved now he'd taken charge. He'd even gone as far as saying that I was "the most exciting prospect in British soccer" and that I "should be groomed to take over Bobby Charlton's role as midfield general of the England team".

So, on a bitterly cold night at the end of October at Wembley I made my full England debut in an important European Championship qualifier against Czechoslovakia.

I was on the bench. Just how cold was I? Well, reports at the time suggested it would have taken me a while to get stripped for action. Under my tracksuit I had a woolly jumper, and to keep my hands warm I sported a pair of goalkeeper Peter Shilton's spare gloves. When I got the call to get prepared and come on I wasn't nervous. I was actually more nervous when I played for England Schoolboys at Wembley as, back then, I wasn't used to playing in front of a large crowd.

It felt like a big night for new England boss Don Revie. There was a crowd of 86,000 inside Wembley wondering what the future held. It was a fresh start and England came out in their new kit, manufactured by Admiral. I'm told that shirt was the first to be commercially available to the public. The age of the replica shirt was upon us. And, judging by the positive result and press we got that night, those shirts must have sold quite well in the aftermath of a strong 3-0 victory. Czechoslovakia, though, were no mugs, as we would find out much later.

The game was a hugely frustrating one to begin with. Like the famous recent draw against Poland that scuppered our World Cup qualification, England couldn't find a way past the resolute Czechs. But even the hard-to-please press reporters who would herald Don Revie's revival of England's football fortunes admitted that this was one special night.

The *Daily Mail*'s Jeff Powell wrote: "By the end Revie had stage-managed the rout of the Czechs with all the showman's flair which he had used to bring Wembley to boiling expectancy."

My moment came in the 65th minute. West Ham's Trevor Brooking and I were the substitutes sent on to change things, and within five minutes of replacing Frank Worthington and Martin Dobson England were in front.

When I came on I couldn't get the ball quick enough. Don Revie had told me to take on their left-back Varadin, and he chopped me down the first two times I went at him. The second time he fouled me I took the resulting free kick and Mick Channon got on the end of it with a brilliantly timed run and headed the ball past the Czech goalkeeper.

That began a fantastic spell where we scored three times in 11 minutes.

After the final whistle I think one of the Czech lads asked me to swap shirts. No disrespect, but I wasn't going to do that. And I've still got that shirt I wore on my debut, and a few others in my bottom drawer.

After the game I celebrated in true Dave Thomas style with my brother, dad and Brenda. No champagne for me - I'd have ordered a hot chocolate.

Obviously, the next day I read all the newspapers. The reports of the game were all very positive.

For a few days there was a bit more press interest in me

as a player. Enough for the *Daily Mirror* to send their famous photographer Monte Fresco to my home in Wokingham to undertake a photo shoot involving me, Brenda and Helen.

I should add that not once when we lived in Wokingham for all those years did I ever have to buy a newspaper. Our next-door neighbour, Fred Warren, was a print worker for the *Daily Express* and he worked night shifts up in London. Fred would return home in the early hours of the morning and by five o'clock there would be a bundle of all the newspapers on our carpet by the front door.

With one headline blaring out "Sub Thomas Torpedoes Czechs" I was on cloud nine, but we all came down to earth with a bump when England played Portugal in another Nations Cup match at Wembley a month later. The press literally gave us the "thumbs down" as we laboured to score in a 0-0 draw.

I was in the starting eleven that night, but it was a frustrating experience made worse by the fact that I was convinced we had scored in the 18th minute. With modern-day technology perhaps we would have won that game when Allan Clarke's shot was clawed out from behind the goal line. From my position a few feet away it looked in, but the officials that night thought otherwise, and at the end of the game the Wembley crowd chanted "What a load of rubbish!"

Already I had experienced one high and a low playing for England.

I took great pride in the fact that I was fortunate enough to play for England at every level. It certainly wasn't easy playing at this new level, but I began to fit in to the routine of international call-ups.

We'd all report to the Hadley Wood Hotel near Cockfosters, which was the meeting point for all the Wembley games. For away

Playing for England Schoolboys and scoring the
winner against West Germany in front of 92,000 at
Wembley in 1966: I think whenever I sum up my
football career, that was probably one of the biggest
highlights. (Photo: S E Taylor)

ABOVE: 'Ticer' and 'Ticer': My grandad's nickname stuck with me too. Here we are in the field behind our house, ready for another training session.

RIGHT: My grandad 'Ticer' Thomas with the Sir Thomas Lipton Trophy he and the West Auckland miners brought home from Italy. (Photo: Ernie Johnson)

BELOW: The statue in West Auckland commemorating grandad's World Cup win. (Photo: David Roberts)

ABOVE: St. Helens Junior School team, with me middle front.
BELOW: I was playing for the Bishop Auckland District team - I'm second from the right in the front row - when Don Revie came to watch me play.

School could be fun:
ABOVE: Here I am towards
the end of my time at Barnard
Castle Secondary Modern
School.
RIGHT: My mate Michael
Taylor (left) and I enjoyed
acting in the school
productions. Here we are
playing Horace and Willie in
The Parker Plan.

ABOVE: Docherty, Probert, Kindon, me, Cliff, Wrigley, West and Jones: FA Youth Cup winners for Burnley in 1968.
BELOW: My debut team photo with the Burnley first XI. Pity about the socks!

ABOVE: with my Burnley room-mate Ralph Coates. Another England international scouted from the north-east and 'made in Lancashire'. BELOW: Whenever I had time, I'd try to get back home to West Auckland to visit mum and dad and brother Melvin. (Photo: J W Henderson)

Socks rolled down and without shin pads. It was never the fashion statement some people thought it was. I just felt more comfortable that way. My boots preference was always for rubbers without studs too. I think Jimmy Greaves was another who played in moulded studs and he didn't do too badly, did he?

December 1972: The day I married
Brenda Blackbell I was literally
rendered speechless! (Photo:
Saxons of Sunderland)

games we would gather at the big Post House off the M4 near Heathrow Airport. My room-mate with England was big Dave Watson. Dave was the top centre half in the country at the time. A lovely lad and coincidentally, like me, born in Nottinghamshire and remembered most for his fantastic performances for Sunderland, which included their legendary cup final victory over Leeds United.

Whenever we arrived at the England hotel, Don Revie, Bill Taylor and Les Cocker were always there to greet you before you checked into your room.

Revie had some unusual ideas. Apart from getting everyone to play bingo - something he'd introduced to his Leeds players for pre-match entertainment - he used to give us each a dossier on our opponents. "Take it to bed with you and read it," he'd say. You can imagine what most of the players did with that! Some would take one look and then tear it up when Revie wasn't looking. But the Leeds players absolutely loved him and his methods certainly worked there.

It was quite tough as a new boy fitting in to the set-up. Although I'd played against all my new England team-mates, I didn't really know any of them at all well. And there were certainly little cliques in the England changing room. Mick Channon, Alan Ball, Emlyn Hughes, Kevin Keegan, Peter Shilton and Ray Clemence had enjoyed much more success than us new lads. There were a lot of established names in that squad. You never felt as if you were welcomed into their world. It was difficult. They were okay with you - don't get me wrong - but they were big card players and I didn't like that sort of thing. Another aspect that made life difficult for us new lads was that Don Revie made Gerry Francis captain. That didn't go down well with some of the old guard. I don't think I was ever properly accepted by some of the older pros in the squad, but I just played my natural, normal game and enjoyed myself.

One player who didn't last long in that England squad was Alan Hudson. Against West Germany in a friendly in April 1975 I was sub, but it gave me the opportunity to watch Alan's debut for England. He'd always impressed me at Under-23 level, but now at full international level he was magnificent. Franz Beckenbauer was playing for the Germans that night but Hudson ran the show. He was selected - alongside me - for the next match, a 5-0 thrashing of Cyprus in a European Championship qualifier, but never again.

Alan had tough times and, coincidentally, I think he eventually went to live in Cyprus. He had more than his fair share of tragedy. He was involved in a terrible car accident. A vehicle hit him while he was out walking and dragged him along. He was in a coma after that. I always thought he was a nice lad and very respectful towards me.

Why did he not go on to get 50 or 60 caps for England? He was, on his day, one of the best I've played against when he was at Chelsea and Stoke City and he so impressed me when playing and training with England.

I have happy memories of my time with England, but it was hard to top that opening win against Czechoslovakia. Our qualifying group began well and ended badly. We lost away to the Czechs in a rough-house of a game. It was an unhappy experience. We were actually leading 1-0 against the Czechs when the fog caused the game to be abandoned after only 17 minutes. The game was then rescheduled for the following day, and again we led before the Czechs equalised just before half-time and scored what turned out to be the winner within a minute of the restart. This time Dave Watson and I were the second-half subs, but there was to be no grandstand finish this time.

Czechoslovakia qualified for the 1976 summer European Championships and won the tournament. After eight caps, I never played for England again.

CHAPTER 10

Sexton: Best Coach I Ever Played For

Under new boss Dave Sexton, QPR's form improved as the 1974/75 season wore on. One victory that must have given Dave some private satisfaction saw us convincingly beat his old employers Chelsea 3-0 at Stamford Bridge. That Chelsea side were relegated at the end of the campaign - a season that saw Derby County, managed by Dave Mackay, finish as league champions. Perhaps our best result that season was against those rampant Rams, who we dispatched 4-1 at Loftus Road, with me opening the scoring.

Some of the training at QPR might surprise you. Near to the ground was an athletics club and we would use their running track. We were coached by a Welsh guy called Ron Jones, who was captain of the British Olympic team. He was our fastest sprinter at the time. Ron worked for a marketing company called Plesseys, but Rangers used to pay him to come along to training. We'd never see a ball, but we loved it. To get people like Stan

Bowles to run was unique! But even 'Bowlesy' enjoyed it. We'd split up into groups, and one particular day I had a lad called John O'Rourke doing the sprints with me. Now John was quite money-orientated, and after one session on the track we got chatting about my time at Burnley.

"When Burnley got promoted the season you came here, did you play any games for them?" he asked. I told John I'd played ten matches at the start of the season before my transfer to Rangers. Burnley boss Jimmy Adamson probably hated picking me, but I was playing really well up to my transfer.

Then John went on to say, "You do know that if you get promoted you get a bonus?"

"But I left the club," I replied.

I didn't get a bonus. But it set me wondering.

Well, if it hadn't been for John O'Rourke I wouldn't have made enquiries.

Our QPR union rep was Terry Venables, so I said to 'Venners', "'Rookers' told me I might have been due a bonus when Burnley got promoted the season Rangers also went up."

I didn't really see it that way, though. I'd left in October after playing ten games. But 'Venners' insisted I give him chapter and verse on the whole situation. So, I told him that for every game you played at Burnley there was a bonus at the end of the season if you got promoted.

That bonus was £125 per game so that was £4,500 extra on top of your wage and appearance money if you'd played all 42 league matches. That was a lot of money in the early '70s. I'd played ten matches, which amounted to £1,250. After I'd explained all this to 'Venners' he got in touch with Cliff Lloyd at the Professional Footballers' Association.

"Dave might have a bit of a case," 'Venners' told Cliff.

Next thing I know, 'Venners' tells me that Cliff Lloyd has rung Albert Maddox at Burnley Football Club and said, "I think you and Bob Lord might owe David Thomas some bonus money for the games he played."

Well, you can imagine their response: "We don't owe him anything!"

And back and forth the conversation went.

"He's entitled."

"No he isn't! He's left the club!"

Anyway, as a result - hardly surprising - there was no agreement...

Then 'Venners' gives me the news one day at training: "Your claim's going to a tribunal Dave."

I couldn't believe it.

"We're going to the Great Western Hotel, near Paddington Station in London," 'Venners' continued, while smiling that ever-present smile of his.

How appropriate, I thought - that's where my Burnley team would stay on trips south.

Obviously, on the day of the tribunal I'm absolutely bricking it.

There's me and wide boy 'Venners' and Bob Lord, Albert Maddox and Jimmy Adamson, who had all made the journey down from Burnley. We're all at the hotel to get the verdict, standing in front of the FA's Harold Thompson, waiting to hear the outcome.

And then Thompson speaks.

"Mr Lord, Mr Maddox and Mr Adamson. We've come to a final decision on David Thomas' £1,250."

Then a long pause. "And the verdict is... that you have to pay it to him."

At that, 'Venners' grabbed me by the arm, jumped up in the air and let out a yell: "Yes!!!"

It took a moment or two for me to comprehend that we had won. Then it was time to take the piss.

With huge grins on our faces we backed out of the room, politely saying, "Thank you very much Mr Thompson. Thank you very much Mr Lord. Thank you very much Mr Maddox and thank you very much Mr Adamson."

So, I come out of the hotel twelve-hundred-and-fifty quid richer and I give my thanks to 'Venners'. What a result!

I wanted to show Terry just how grateful I was.

Then I had an idea.

"Brenda and I would like to take you and your wife out to dinner to celebrate. Can you book somewhere, because we don't know London like you do. Please make it somewhere special… and we're paying."

Of course, 'Venners' knew everyone and everywhere to go, so when Brenda and I returned to meet him and his then-wife Christine, he said, "I've booked the Sportsman's Club."

So, we go in, sit down at a lovely table and 'Venners' orders the drinks. I think it was champagne. But there was to be no fancy food for him. I'll never forget it. He calls over another waiter and orders liver and bacon!

We then enjoy a wonderful celebration meal and have a great time. But the evening was about to get more surreal. As Terry Venables was finishing his liver and bacon, Brenda nudged me and said, "David, have you seen who's over there?"

And then I spot who it is and start pointing him out to 'Venners'. "Look! Look! It's Percy Thrower!"

And there, over on the gaming tables, is one of my gardening heroes: Percy Thrower. It really *is* Percy Thrower.

"'Venners'," I say, "I can't believe this! I watch him on TV every week on *Gardeners' World*!

I'm not joking. There was Percy Thrower, in a club full of glamorous people, playing roulette with a pile of chips in front of him.

So, of course, 'Venners' says, "Do you want to meet him?" And then he proceeds to introduce me.

Well, after that Percy Thrower went down in my estimation! I couldn't believe it was the same man. Unbelievable.

***

If playing in the top division under Gordon Jago's coaching had been enjoyable, working with new boss Dave Sexton looked like taking QPR up to another level entirely.

If you asked anyone in the game, Dave Sexton was very well respected. A very quiet and unassuming man, but you wouldn't want to cross him. He came from a boxing family and he could be tough when he needed to be. Before he took over at QPR there were stories about how he kept control at Chelsea. Back then, Chelsea was the club that attracted a number of celebrity supporters and some of the players were like celebrities themselves. Centre forward Peter Osgood was king at Stamford Bridge, but Dave Sexton never took any nonsense from him or anyone else. It's said that he even offered Osgood outside for a fight once after one altercation and Osgood turned him down! Dave could look after himself. As is so often the case, as they say, it's the quiet ones you have to watch.

You can imagine trying to manage Stan Bowles. Nightmare! Well, Stan loved Dave. Stan would come down at ten to three on a Saturday and get changed for the game. No warm-up. He'd have been up in the players' lounge watching the racing on television. If Dave had been the sort of manager who said "I want you here at half past two for the team meeting without fail" it wouldn't have worked. Dave never said a word to Stan. When he'd finally make an appearance shortly before kick-off, the players were fine with it because you always knew when Stan went out, he'd give 110 per cent.

He'd also come in late for training on numerous occasions, always in a rush, always in a taxi (Stan never drove), and again not a word from Dave or the rest of us. Bizarrely, in Stan's autobiography he claimed to have driven me to training. Unbelievable!

Okay, in truth, we did all moan about him! All good fun. But come Saturday 'Bowlesy' would always do the business.

Stan was like Alan Hudson in some respects. I always felt that when they were away from football, that's when they had their problems. Stan felt safe when he was on the pitch. He was always happy when he was training or playing matches. Stan's problems materialised when he had time on his hands. He had a lot of so-called friends. What an odd bunch of people - more hangers-on - they were. Gambling, ducking and diving, that was Stan's approach to life. He regularly owed money to certain people, but when he was on the pitch they couldn't get to him. He was married and with three children. But you couldn't imagine Stan going home after a game, having dinner with the family and putting the TV on and watching *Match of the Day*! He'd be off to the dogs at White City. He loved greyhound racing.

Don Shanks and Stan were the biggest gamblers at the club. When 'Bowlesy' separated from his wife, he and Shanks shared a flat together in Shepherd's Bush. They were always behind with the rent and owed money to everyone.

One Shanks and Stan story Rangers fans may have heard before starts with a knock on the flat door. It's the landlady. Shanks opens the door and says, "Yes? Can I help you?" And the landlady says, "Yes. I'm looking for the rent."

Shanks replies, "You'd better come in love and we'll all look for it!"

'Bowlesy' and Shanks got kicked out of the flat after that.

They were always up to mischief. Dave Clement, our right-back, and Mick Leach were down to open a local supermarket once, and for whatever reason couldn't make it. Ever the opportunists, 'Bowlesy' and 'Shanksy' took their places without even telling Dave and Mick and hired a van. Apparently, the supermarket manager had told them that instead of a fee for their services they could help themselves to some of the store's goods. Well, the two of them filled up the van and probably flogged the contents on. From what I heard, they nearly cleaned out that supermarket! True story.

How Dave Sexton kept control of our squad I don't know. It couldn't have been easy, but he managed us superbly. My only criticism might be that he wasn't interested in contracts or any money-orientated business of that kind. He didn't appreciate the confrontation when players knock on the manager's door. That wasn't his scene at all. Directing operations on the training pitch was his thing. I got the impression Dave would have worked for nothing. He was a terrific coach. All he wanted was to make you a better player.

We already had some really good players at QPR. Bowles and Venables had been spotted and brought in by Gordon Jago. Frank McLintock from Arsenal, Dave Webb and John Hollins from Chelsea and Don Masson from Notts County had been added to the mix. And what additions they had proved to be. Dave Webb was a wheeler-dealer and was always trying to earn a few quid outside of football. Want a fridge or a car? See Dave. Not a great trainer, but what an amazing player on the pitch. I absolutely loved him. He was hard as nails and very tough, but surprisingly very quiet. The character of the man was best illustrated by that famous FA Cup final he played in when Leeds and Chelsea drew at Wembley. Eddie Gray absolutely slaughtered him that day. A lot of players wouldn't have fancied defending against Gray again, but in the replay at Old Trafford Dave had the last laugh and scored the memorable winning goal from that huge Ian Hutchinson long throw.

The McLintock signing was a particular coup. How did QPR manage that? Well let's just say the chairman was very creative with that deal! Money talks, doesn't it? Jim Gregory was a likeable rogue in that respect.

I can't imagine there were many dressing rooms as lively as ours. The banter between us players was always good, but the team comedian might surprise you. Johnny Hollins was hilarious. Ian Gillard used to love him. He was also a very switched-on guy and perfected the art of the funny one-liner - mostly piss-taking one-liners at the expense of one of his team-mates.

The wonderful team spirit wasn't just confined to the players. One great memory of Dave Sexton comes to mind instantly. We used to go to a training camp in Germany called 'Heliff'. A German Second Division side called Fortuna Cologne were training at the same time and they were using those dummies on springs to practise taking free kicks against them. Quite new in those days, I think. Dave saw those German dummies and went up to their coach and bought the lot. So, we transported them back to England through customs. Once our plane had landed, the German dummies all went on the conveyor belt and we paid the excess on baggage!

Every month, out of his own pocket, Dave Sexton would pay for a prize for the best player in the squad that month. If you won, you'd have the choice of an inscribed carriage clock, cigarette lighter or a suitcase. I've still got my inscribed carriage clock! You can see why we loved working with him.

Although we had been struggling for points until his arrival in October, at the end of Dave's first season in charge we ended with a 3-1 defeat at Liverpool and finished in 11th place. The 1975/76 campaign that followed would see us kick off against Liverpool at home. It would be Queens Park Rangers' best-ever season.

CHAPTER 11

The Race for the League Title

The season we almost won the league got off to the best possible start when we beat what most people thought was the top team back then, Liverpool. Gerry Francis and Mick Leach got the goals in a 2-0 win and we absolutely pummelled them.

A week later we were really flying. It wasn't the first time we had given Dave Mackay's Derby County a good beating. This time they were reigning champions and we ran out 5-1 winners at the Baseball Ground against a line-up that's worth listing: Colin Boulton, Colin Todd, Rod Thomas, David Nish, Roy McFarland, Kevin Hector, Bruce Rioch, Archie Gemmill, Henry Newton, Charlie George and Francis Lee. Our goals that Saturday were from a hat-trick courtesy of 'Bowlesy', one from Dave Clement and one from me.

We managed five again a couple of months later at home to Everton. This victory was achieved without 'Bowlesy' this time,

111

with Francis (2), Givens, Masson and me finding the back of the net.

We were playing some wonderful stuff. We seemed to be always on *The Big Match* and were London football's top attraction. We were winning games emphatically, and results like the 3-0 victory away at Spurs made people sit up and take notice.

As the season wore on, it became clear to us that we were good enough to win the league. Any Rangers fans lucky enough to have been following the club back in 1976 will recall the nail-biting finish we endured.

We had to win our last three games to be crowned champions. But on the Saturday over Easter we got beaten 3-2 away at Norwich City. I scored an equaliser to drag us back into the game at 1-1, but a controversial goal from the home team did for us that day.

The pressure was really on then in our two final games, which were thankfully at Loftus Road. Again, we were a goal down to Arsenal on Easter Monday. Incredibly, we had been forced to come from behind four games in a row. On this occasion a former Gunner and now our centre half, Frank McLintock, equalised for us and then Gerry Francis scored what turned out to be the winner from the penalty spot.

So, on Saturday the 24th of April, we kicked off our last game of the season in front of our second full house that week. Leeds United were the visitors, and with the likes of Joe Jordan, Billy Bremner and Norman Hunter in their line-up we knew that if we were going to have any chance of winning the league title we would be doing it the hard way.

I don't remember many of the goals I scored in my career - I wasn't exactly prolific - but I do remember two from that season. One was a special long-range effort in the League Cup at

Charlton Athletic earlier in the season, and the second that stands out was the opening goal in what turned out to be a 2-0 victory that day against Leeds. It was a header! As I say, I didn't score many and very few with my head. We had done all we could, but we then had an excruciating wait to find out whether Liverpool would overtake our points tally in their final game. Their last match, away at high-flying Wolves, was scheduled to take place an astonishing ten days after we'd completed our fixtures.

So QPR Football Club went to the Middle East for an end-of-season tour and played a friendly against Maccabi Tel Aviv. While in the area we visited the Wailing Wall in Jerusalem, and some of us players stuck little notes into it praying for Liverpool not to overtake us!

At least we had some fun and games to keep our minds off the nerve-wracking end to the season back home. Before the end of the trip we were all in the hotel reception area enjoying a drink or two when who should walk in through the hotel doors up to reception? Oscar-winning movie star Jack Palance. Our resident comedian, Johnny Hollins, spotted Mr Palance immediately. 'Hollie', who had probably had more than a drink or two, proceeded to tell the rest of the team, "I'm going up to him - I'm going to introduce myself."

And that's exactly what he did, calling out excitedly: "All right Jack? How you doing?!"

Palance slowly turned round, and with a straight face said, "Why don't you just fuck off?" before nonchalantly walking into the lift with his film crew in tow.

And there's Hollins, stood there with his arms wide open, as if to say, "Well okay. If you don't want to know me…"

We did laugh!

That wasn't the only funny incident I remember from that

tour. Dave Webb loved a cigar, and if the lads were out of the hotel at a club or socialising in the hotel bar, Dave would settle down quietly in a comfortable chair with a drink and smoke his cigar. One night there was a British guy causing a bit of grief. I think he'd had a few drinks and was giving us plenty of chat. I can recall, as clear as anything, Dave just saying, "This guy is properly getting on my nerves."

Dave didn't swear, didn't shout, and added, "I think somebody better get this guy out of here."

Then he put down his drink, puffed on his cigar and quietly got to his feet and hit the bloke hard once and laid him out on the floor. Dave sat down again, picked up his cigar and quietly began puffing away again and sipping his drink. Ice-cool and strong as an ox was Dave.

What on earth he would have been like if he ever got *really* mad or angry with someone I dread to think.

On my return to England from our trip to the Middle East, I was invited to add to the commentary on BBC radio for the Wolves v Liverpool game at Molineux that would decide our fate. Don Howe and I were in the BBC studios in London.

I'm sure the tension must have been great for those Liverpool players, but for us Rangers players all we could do was watch and wait to see if we would be crowned champions. When the game kicked off the tension almost immediately went up a notch. Incredibly there was to be another twist in the story. My old Burnley mate Steve Kindon opened the scoring with a goal for Wolves. But, sadly, back came Liverpool to eventually win 3-1 and take the title with goals from Ray Kennedy, Kevin Keegan and John Toshack.

Liverpool were champions and we were runners-up. But

I think that QPR team will always be remembered for playing great football.

It was a special time in my career, playing with a special bunch of lads.

CHAPTER 12
QPR in Europe

The following season we failed to reach the heights of the previous one in the league, but we did have European football at Loftus Road for the first time. As league runners-up in 1976, QPR entered the UEFA Cup for the 1976/77 season. It was the club's first experience of European competition - and mine - in club football. I think the way we played in those days was suited to continental football. We played a very rigid 4-3-3 and tactically Dave Sexton was very aware of our foreign opponents. After our league games at weekends, he would always rush off to Germany and Holland to watch games over there. And Dave had us playing out from the back, so it was perfect for our UEFA Cup campaign.

We started really well, and I think the 11-0 thrashing on aggregate of Norway's SK Brann in the first round set us up with confidence. Next were Czech side Slovan Bratislava, who we beat 8-5 over both legs. A 4-4 aggregate, with us going through on away goals against FC Cologne of West Germany, took us to a place in the quarter-finals, where we were drawn against AEK Athens of Greece.

All the other English teams - Manchester United, Manchester City and Derby County - had already been knocked out of the UEFA Cup that season, so it was a big deal for us. I'll never forget the first leg, under the lights at Loftus Road. The little stadium was absolutely heaving with people. Packed to the rafters. Our chairman, Jim Gregory, had come up with a bonus scheme for us players based on a certain percentage of the attendances over 20,000, I think it was. As a result, if we attracted a crowd of 25,000 we would get a percentage of the extra 5,000 or something like that. Anyway, we beat AEK Athens 3-0 at Loftus Road in a wonderful atmosphere that night. We had the day off after the game and we all naturally read the papers the following morning.

Imagine our surprise when we saw the gate reported as only 18,000! Jim Gregory, it would appear, had fixed the gate so that there was no player bonus. It felt like there must have been 30,000 in the ground. Anyway, some of the senior players, including captain Gerry Francis, had a meeting with Jim and eventually he came around to our way of thinking. Typical Jim Gregory that was.

The drama in the second leg in Greece was far more scary. As our team coach approached the AEK Athens ground, we could all see they had attracted a massive crowd. Inside their stadium, they had a moat all around the pitch. As I had failed a fitness test I didn't actually play in that match, so I was sitting in the dugout. Close to the AEK fans, I could appreciate just how scary the atmosphere was that night. The first time I looked over my shoulder at the crowd I noticed a guy behind me. He had a knife and he was threatening us with it, quite openly. Thank goodness for that moat!

As far as the match was concerned, we were 3-0 down at the final whistle so the game went into extra time and then penalties. I think it was David Webb who missed the crucial penalty for us and we were out of the competition. Getting away from the stadium wasn't easy after the game either. Despite the fact that AEK Athens had won and were in the semi-finals, the atmosphere was still very threatening. Large crowds surrounded our team bus and there didn't seem to be much in the way of security. I look back on that campaign and recall it being an incredible experience, but, certainly in Greece, it also became a frightening one.

We'd done well - we were the last English team to get knocked out of the UEFA Cup that season and our cup exploits outshone our league form.

Although I was sidelined at the time, once again in the league we had a memorable win against Tommy Docherty's Manchester United. We continued our 100% winning form against them at Loftus Road and thumped them 4-0 this time. The goal-scorers that day in March were perhaps an indication of just how much the QPR team was changing at that time. On the scoresheet were Don Givens, Eddie Kelly and two for Peter Eastoe.

That season I nearly made a Wembley final again. We had a good run in the League Cup but, just as I'd done at Burnley, we came a cropper in the semi-final, this time against Aston Villa. Once again it was over two legs and both games were draws, and unbelievably again, because there were no penalty shoot-outs in those days, we had to play a third game. This time we thought we had some kind of edge over our rivals. Our trump card was likeable rogue Jim Gregory, the QPR chairman. Gregory and

Doug Ellis, his opposite number at Villa, tossed a coin to see who had the choice of a neutral ground. Apparently, Gregory tossed the coin and it span under the table and out of view. Gregory immediately dived on the coin and called out "It's tails" and "We choose."

Great you would have thought - advantage QPR. Well, as a result of Gregory winning the toss, we took Villa down to the nearby Highbury stadium and they beat us 3-0. Those Burnley v Swindon and QPR v Aston Villa three-game marathons were the closest I came to a Wembley final.

At the end of the season there was to be another career change for me - an unexpected one. I'd just signed a new deal with Rangers. But then Dave Sexton left to take over the manager's seat at Old Trafford after Tommy Docherty had been sacked by Manchester United. Frank Sibley took over from Dave. It was a special moment for Frank. He was a favourite of the chairman. He'd trained the reserves, had been a team-mate to some of us and it was his time to step up. One of his first jobs was to ring me. I was at home in Wokingham and the call came right out of the blue. I was happily settled at QPR, so I had no thoughts about starting a new season playing for anyone other than Rangers.

"David," he said, "the choice is yours, and I know you've just signed a four-year contract, but Everton have put in a bid for you."

Obviously I was surprised, but Frank went on to say, "I want you to stay, but I think the powers that be want to sell you."

CHAPTER 13

Out of the Blue: Everton Come Calling

Having just signed a new contract, I hadn't expected to make any kind of decision about my future that summer, but I did have an inkling that the team Dave Sexton was leaving behind was maybe going to break up.

Having talked over the implications of a move back up north with Brenda, I decided I'd drive up to Everton to meet Gordon Lee, their manager. Gordon had only been at the club since January, having previously been in charge at Newcastle United. The meeting went well, and after their secretary Jim Greenwood had offered me a contract, I ended up signing for Everton Football Club for a fee of £225,000. *Daily Mirror* reports suggested Everton had had to fight off a rival bid from Newcastle United, Gordon Lee's former employers, but that was news to me.

On the same day I signed, Everton also brought in a Scottish goalkeeper, George Wood, from Blackpool. Nice lad George, and a great acquisition as it turned out. As he and I began our time at Everton together, we car-shared to training and became part of a great bunch of lads at the club. Striker Duncan McKenzie was one of them. He took me all over the local area to show me places to live. He was very helpful and I was grateful for that.

Just three days after signing I made my Everton debut at Goodison Park against Brian Clough's Nottingham Forest. It was the season they would go on to win the league and they beat us 3-1. Then we went to Arsenal in midweek and we lost again. I thought, 'Blimey, this is going to be a tough old season.'

Looking back, the turning point would appear to have come in our third game - away to Aston Villa - where we came from behind to snatch a 2-1 win, Duncan McKenzie scoring both goals.

Everything clicked and we went on a terrific run of 18 league games unbeaten until we were thumped 6-2 at Goodison Park on Boxing Day by Manchester United. Mind you, that season we handed out a few thrashings of our own. In September I managed a rare goal in a 5-1 win at Leicester City. November saw us slaughter Coventry City 6-0 at Goodison, a score we repeated against Chelsea on the final day of the season. When you are winning, confidence just grows and grows and the side really gelled together.

My special partnership with centre forward Bob Latchford was wonderful. Although all throughout my professional career team-mates would nickname me 'Ticer' - just like my grandad - Bob always called me 'Tizer'. Because I was bubbly he'd say. Just like the famous bottle of pop back then.

I found out while I was at Everton that Bob had remembered seeing me play at Wembley as a schoolboy international. After that he and I actually played together for the England Under-19 team in East Germany in 1969.

'Latch' and I were always looking for each other on the pitch at Everton. Almost immediately the goals started to flow.

Of all the big scores we racked up that memorable season, the one that sticks out most was my return to Loftus Road in October. The home fans were lovely. No boos for me. They were incredibly respectful. The score that afternoon was QPR 1 Everton 5, with Bob scoring four. Quite a high proportion of his goals came from my crosses. 'Latch' was a typical goalscorer. He was brave and very powerful, but off the pitch a very quiet, humble guy.

I loved this quote from him after he retired: "Dixie [Dean] scored sixty goals in a season - I scored thirty. If Evertonians remember me as being only half as good as that great man I'd be very happy."

These days Bob lives near Nuremberg in Germany, but still heads back to England from time to time for Everton player reunions. He had that knack of coming alive in the box. Bob knew if I got a yard on my defender I'd never check or come back. I'd get the ball in early, and from every opportunity I got I wouldn't hesitate to get it into the box for him. In today's game, what infuriates me is when I see a player going to the byline and then stop and pass the ball back. Sometimes a positive move like that ends up with a passing move that sees the ball going back to the goalkeeper. God gave me a gift to beat my man and deliver the ball at height. Crosses should never hit the first defender. It's just me getting old and cynical! But there is too much reliance on playing the ball on the ground these days. There was never any danger I was going to do that with Bob Latchford in our side. In my day, defenders always preferred the ball on the ground to in the air.

In my first season at Everton, we finished third behind champions

Nottingham Forest and runners-up Liverpool. Although we had only managed one point from the two Merseyside derbies that season, the final league table only showed a two-point gap between us and the team from the other side of Stanley Park.

My switch to Everton showed yet again how differently clubs operate. The club was very well organised - a class act. John Moores was the chairman and the whole board of directors, like him, had a great deal of style. QPR was a bit backwards in comparison. The Everton training ground was immaculate, and the facilities were ten years ahead of anyone else. Walled gardens. Walled training ground. Security gates. And Everton were one of the first clubs to introduce lunch in a canteen after training. You could have a three-course meal if you wanted it.

Another innovation was that some of the Everton lads used to go to a hotel on a Friday to get away from family distractions. It probably made sense. Throughout my career, Brenda would see my character change on a Thursday. I'd be starting to think about Saturday's match at that point.

The Goodison Park crowds were noticeably bigger and much noisier than most. I'd always enjoyed playing at Old Trafford and Anfield. As a former Everton player I probably shouldn't say it, but Anfield had an incredibly special atmosphere on match days. The Kop end was literally rocking on occasions. Both Old Trafford and Anfield were big stadiums, but you always felt the crowd were close to you. It was the same at Goodison and was also the case at Loftus Road, a much smaller ground where night matches had been electric. As a winger you maybe notice these things more as you are mostly standing nearer to someone in the crowd than you are to some of your team-mates. In the '70s there were a few grounds where I felt less in touch with the crowd if there was a running track. These were the grounds where I sometimes needed to psych myself up a little bit more to get going. Watford's Vicarage Road ground was one example. They had a greyhound track running around the pitch and the atmosphere there was terrible. I understand that when Graham Taylor was first appointed manager there by Elton John, his first important decision was to request the greyhound track was scrapped and the stadium has changed out of all recognition these days. Being close to the crowd did have its disadvantages too, of course. It meant any abuse that rained down from the terraces at me was much easier to hear!

Having signed just a few days before the previous season began, I now experienced my first pre-season at Everton. It was as tough as anything I'd encountered before. Occasionally we'd all go off to the sand dunes near Southport on the coast. Running up and down those dunes in the sand was hard. If the training facilities were first class, so were the travel arrangements. Behind the scenes you were taken care of in a way I really appreciated. The club had solicitors and estate agents sorting out everything for us as me, Brenda and the girls moved to the north-west.

The other big difference at Everton was the press interest. It was significantly higher on Merseyside to what I'd come across at Burnley and QPR. In addition to the newspapers there was Radio City and Radio Merseyside. There were two particular reporters I had a lot of time for during my spell at Everton: Martin Leach of the *News of the World* was always good and Richard Keys, who was starting his career at Radio City.

A lot of the footballers were living at Southport, Formby and Ainsdale, but preferring a more rural set-up we ended up living in Parbold, about 20 miles or so north-east of Liverpool. We bought a house in the village and stayed there five years and loved every minute. We really fell on our feet. A big plus was the fact that the local school only had 20 children in it. For our two girls it was like a private education.

As a family we were settled in the area and on the pitch I was too, largely down to the way Gordon Lee managed Everton at the time. Gordon was a lovely man and helped and encouraged me to play at a level that was on a par with my best moments at QPR.

Gordon made us laugh too. When we got knocked out of the FA Cup in January and went on a mid-season break to Majorca, the hotel we stayed in was the Son Vida and it was five-star luxury. As you can imagine it was a bit posh for some of us Everton lads. Also joining us on the trip were John Moores, Philip Carter and a couple of the other directors, and all the coaching staff. Gordon had no flashness about him. A very simple diet suited him. He was always quite happy with pie and peas or fish and chips. If you mentioned a la carte to him, he thought it was a starter.

Gordon always had a habit of going up to the players on a Friday night in the hotel when they were eating their chosen meals and examining what was on their plates.

"Bloody hell! What's that?" he'd say, or "I don't like the look of that!" while looking over the players' shoulders.

Anyway, we all come down for dinner at the Son Vida one evening and physio Jim McGregor was sitting with the directors drinking a nice glass of wine.

He's just about to eat his meal and Gordon starts: "Bloody hell Jim. What's that?"

Jim replies, "Welsh rabbit" and Gordon looks astonished and says, "Fucking hell, looks like cheese on toast to me."

Typical Gordon.

In some ways I'd say my two seasons at Everton were the best years of my playing career. The Latchford and Thomas partnership was a winning formula that both of us thoroughly enjoyed and the goals flowed. My only disappointment was my omission from all the England squads during that period. I half expected the call but it never came, for whatever reason. My own view was that I was playing better than ever, backed by some terrific support.

I've got to say the Everton fans were fantastic. Typical scousers: they really appreciated good football, and if they took to you they were brilliant. I was grateful for that because I knew if they didn't take to you they could make life difficult.

A real fans' favourite during my time at the club was Duncan McKenzie. Duncan was a real character and another one of football's mavericks. Among the lads I played with he was one of the craziest. He went down in football folklore when he jumped over a mini on the pitch as part of the pre-match entertainment for Paul Reaney's testimonial when he was at Leeds United. It was his party trick. Duncan was lovely and particularly welcoming when I first arrived at Everton, but without being too critical he wasn't what you would call a team player. We could get beat 4-3 and he'd still pipe up with the fact that he'd scored a hat-trick. "I did my job!" he'd say. It was all about Duncan! But he had massive ability on the ball. It was just a pity he didn't take more care of himself. Health-wise, he was never in the best of shape, and given the opportunity you'd often see him smoking. Duncan loved a cigarette. Bought by the previous Everton manager Billy Bingham, when Lee became manager Duncan wasn't Gordon's sort of player and he eventually sold him to Chelsea. Shortly after Duncan left, another fans' favourite wrote himself into Everton folklore.

Andy King was very much Gordon's sort of player.

If you told 'Kingy' to jump off of the Forth Bridge he'd jump. He was easily led! Our affectionate nickname for him was 'tit-head'! Daft as a bloody brush, but a brilliant, lovely lad with a heart of gold. He'd get up to all sorts - dropping his shorts and mooning on a golf course, liked a flutter on the horses. Everton fans and his team-mates will never forget the memories he gave them. One big memory stands out above the rest.

We played Liverpool at Goodison Park in October 1978 and, for the first time in seven years, Everton won the Merseyside derby. Andy scored the spectacular only goal that day, on a sunlit afternoon I'll never forget. Neither will the blue half of Merseyside. It was a big win by any standards as neither side had lost a match in the run-up to the game. I would have made it 2-0 but for a dramatic clearance off the line by Alan Hansen. But it was Andy's day. At the end of the game we are all celebrating on the pitch and 'Kingy' is trying to do an interview for the BBC, surrounded by Everton fans, when a uniformed policeman grabs him by the arm and says, "Excuse me - get off the pitch" - bundling our hero away from the cameras. Check it out on YouTube. Hilarious!

Another player in that Merseyside derby who had a really big impact on me was Colin Todd. Colin had only recently signed for Everton from Derby County. Colin was probably the most naturally gifted footballer I played with. Fantastic defender: so quick, very few got past him. 'Toddy' was also an example of a guy who really surprised me when he hung up his boots and went into management. He was always a dedicated professional, but when training was done or a game was over he would always head straight home.

The Everton lad I spent most time with was left-back Mike Pejic. Mike was an amazing character - one I got to know pretty

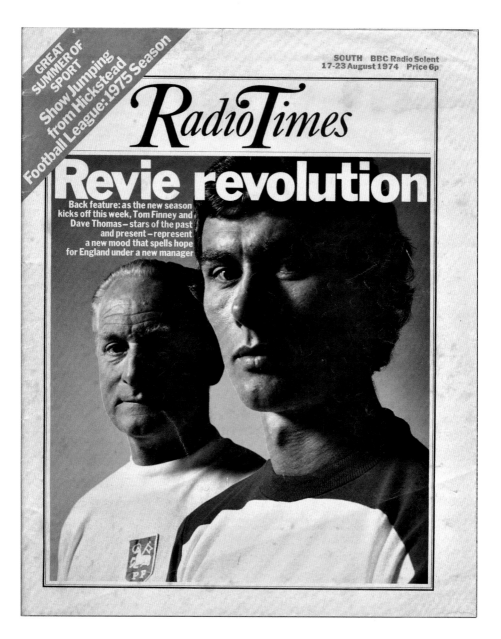

SOUTH   BBC Radio Solent
17-23 August 1974   Price 6p

GREAT SUMMER OF SPORT
Show Jumping from Hickstead
Football League: 1975 Season

RadioTimes

Revie revolution

Back feature: as the new season kicks off this week, Tom Finney and Dave Thomas – stars of the past and present – represent a new mood that spells hope for England under a new manager

With the new season about to kick off in August 1974, I nominated Tom Finney as my hero for a *Radio Time*s feature about the future of the England team under new manager Don Revie. (Photo: Allan Ballard)

In action home
(v Nottingham
Forest, above) and
away (v Ipswich
Town, left) for the
'Super Hoops'.

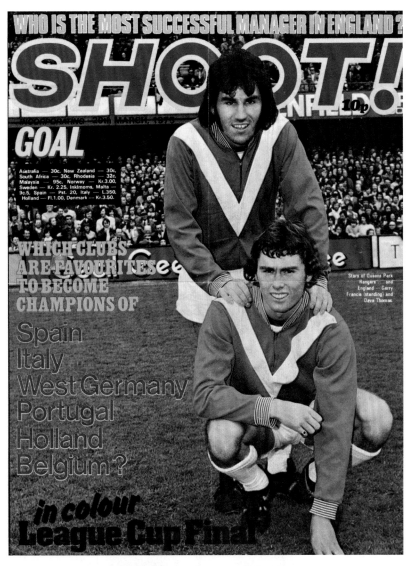

ABOVE: QPR cover boys: me and Gerry Francis in March 1975.

LEFT: Brenda and I celebrate my England call-up as a full international. (Photo: Evening Post)

At home in Wokingham, with Brenda, Helen and Polly.

LEFT: Enjoying a pot of tea and a joke at the England team hotel with Tony Towers, Mick Channon and Gerry Francis. (Photo: *The Sun*)

BELOW: Sharing the back page with George Best on the August day in 1977 I signed for Everton.

FOCUS ON

DAVE THOMAS
Everton

FULL NAME: Dave Thomas
BIRTHPLACE: Kirkby-in-Ashfield
BIRTHDATE: 5th October, 1950
HEIGHT: 5ft 8ins
WEIGHT: 11st 8lbs
PREVIOUS CLUBS: Burnley and Queens Park Rangers
MARRIED: Yes
CHILDREN: Two, Helen and Polly Jane
CAR: Lancia
FAVOURITE PLAYER: None
FAVOURITE OTHER TEAM: None
MOST DIFFICULT OPPONENT: They're all difficult
MOST MEMORABLE MATCH: Debut for England v. Czechoslovakia at Wembley, October, 1974
BIGGEST THRILL: Scoring winning goal for England schoolboys at Wembley
BIGGEST DISAPPOINTMENTS: Losing in two League Cup Semi-Finals
BEST COUNTRY VISITED: Norway
FAVOURITE FOOD: Steak
MISCELLANEOUS LIKES: Fishing and gardening
MISCELLANEOUS DISLIKES: People who aren't punctual
FAVOURITE TV SHOW: World About Us and all gardening programmes
FAVOURITE SINGERS: None
FAVOURITE ACTORS: Paul Newman and Clint Eastwood
BIGGEST INFLUENCE ON CAREER: My parents
BIGGEST DRAG IN SOCCER: Injuries
INTERNATIONAL HONOURS: Schoolboy, Youth, Under-23's and Full caps
PERSONAL AMBITION: To be happy
PROFESSIONAL AMBITION: To win something
IF YOU WEREN'T A FOOTBALLER, WHAT DO YOU THINK YOU'D BE? Haven't a clue
WHICH PERSON IN THE WORLD WOULD YOU MOST LIKE TO MEET? Geoffrey Smith, the TV Gardening expert

LEFT: *Shoot!* readers must have been astonished to discover the answer to the final question. "Which person in the world would you most like to meet?" it says. "Easy: Geoffrey Smith, the TV gardening expert!"

RIGHT: I may have only played 16 times for the Vancouver Whitecaps, but our time as a family living in Canada was a lot of fun. I seem to be enjoying myself just as much as the kids at this public soccer coaching day.

RIGHT: Gardening was always a passion, but it also became a career when I left professional football for good.

BELOW MIDDLE: Working alongside commentator Peter Hood at Fratton Park was a very enjoyable experience. (Photo: *Pompey Magazine*)

BELOW: I'm getting more like Stevie Wonder every week! Those lessons from Miss Heslop when I was a kid came in handy. Here I am drawing a small crowd at St. Pancras station.

ABOVE: At home in Lartington with my collection of shirts and caps, which I keep safely under the bed! That's my England cap from a match against Portugal and the shirt I wore on my debut against Czechoslovakia at Wembley in 1974. BELOW: What a wonderful lifeline Hannah has been. She gives me so much confidence and independence. (Photos: David Roberts)

well as he was my Everton room-mate. When I first joined the club, Mike had a hill farm just outside Stoke-on-Trent. He was another lad like 'Toddy' who couldn't wait to get home after training back to his farm. He didn't appear to have much interest in football beyond actually playing and training but, again, surprised us all when he became a full-time FA coaching examiner. I never saw that coming. Mike was also ranked third in the world at taekwondo for his age a few years ago! Windsurfing is another passion of his. What a character. He and I got on so well and I love him to bits. He was my Everton soulmate.

I met up with Mike recently and there's one memory that always comes up when we get chatting about our Everton days. One person Mike never took to was Welsh referee Clive Thomas. He hated him with a passion! Every Evertonian had good cause to list him as their least favourite ref and Mike would never let you forget why Thomas was so unpopular on the blue half of Merseyside.

Mike's rage stemmed from a disallowed goal in the 1977 Everton v Liverpool FA Cup semi-final at Manchester City's old ground, Maine Road. Everton substitute Bryan Hamilton came on and put the ball into the Liverpool net with his thigh. As he was wearing fresh white shorts, everyone could see the muddy mark on his shorts where the ball had come from. The Evertonians never forgave Clive Thomas, who was refereeing that day. It cost Everton the game. If that was controversial, it was nothing compared to the goal he disallowed for Brazil in the World Cup in Argentina a year later. He insisted he had already blown his whistle for full-time as a corner came over and Zico thought he'd scored the winning goal against Sweden. Thinking of another World Cup reminds me that possibly our best referee at the time, Jack Taylor, officiated at the 1974 final between West

Germany and Holland. Jack was very good, and is one of the few who I think could have coped with the modern game. My current favourite is Michael Oliver. Aside from the fact that he's a young north-east lad from Ashington, he gets my vote because he makes his decisions very, very quickly and isn't swayed.

That 1978/79 season, my second at Goodison, started so well. Aside from the big win against Liverpool, we stayed unbeaten in the league until just before Christmas. The only defeats suffered up to that point came in the League Cup, when we were knocked out by Nottingham Forest, and our exit from Europe. Our UEFA Cup journey began by beating Ireland's Finn Harps 5-0 in both legs, but didn't extend beyond a close encounter with Czech team Dukla Prague, who went through on the away goals rule over both legs.

The second half of the season didn't go nearly so well for us. We still managed to finish in fourth place, but were well behind champions Liverpool. I didn't play in the final games of that season and was looking for an improved deal with the club when I got some advice from an unusual source - Bill Shankly.

Liverpool's legendary former manager used to come in to Everton's Bellefield training ground almost every morning. Retirement since he'd left Liverpool in 1974 clearly hadn't suited him. He was a lost soul, he really was. When he was manager across Stanley Park he probably had no time for Everton, but he'd had a little bit of a fall-out with Liverpool Football Club. A directorship that maybe didn't happen? I don't know, but perhaps that role wouldn't have worked. He had possibly too much authority around Anfield for that to work. Now, a few years into his retirement, it was the camaraderie he missed. He'd come in and use the training ground facilities with Everton manager Gordon Lee's blessing. He'd even have a shower there and a cup of tea, and end up chatting with us players and staff. I don't recall him ever watching training on the touchline, but I do vividly recall him in the dressing rooms or deep in conversation with physio Jim McGregor in the treatment room. Some of the Everton players thought he was a pain in the backside, but I loved Bill. He could chat and I could listen to him all day. He used to live around the corner from Bellefield in a little semi-detached house - not flash at all. Typical working-class guy. With that wonderful hard-as-nails Scottish accent he had, he was so interesting to listen to.

When my contract was coming to an end at Everton, I went to see Gordon Lee about my future and to discuss a pay rise. Bless Gordon, he was lovely but he had his hands tied on some issues and I wasn't getting anywhere.

Anyway, I happened to mention to Bill Shankly during one of our chats about all this. I hadn't got an agent and I valued his advice.

'Shanks' said, "Come round to my house one night, son, and we'll talk some more."

I happily took up his offer one evening and called round. Bill's wife Nessie was there. She offered me a cup of tea and left us to our chat. So, I told Bill my situation, including how much I was on a week, which at the time was £300. That was a good wage back then, but when he heard that he got quite animated. "What, £300 a week?! You are worth at least £500. You deserve it, son."

Bill Shankly certainly wasn't materialistic, but he obviously felt Everton were maybe taking advantage of me.

That conversation with Bill prompted me to go back to Gordon Lee and I asked him if he could arrange a meeting with me and whoever made the decisions about improved contracts. He duly did, and I went to see recently appointed chairman Philip Carter at his Littlewoods offices, where he was a director.

I started the meeting nervously: "Mr Carter, I hope you don't mind me asking but I'd like an increase on my contract." Nice man Philip Carter, but he wasn't budging and flatly refused my request.

Obviously, the matter didn't end there. I wasn't the only one in a position where I thought Everton owed me a bit more. Bob Latchford was also in dispute with the club over a new deal. So, Bob and I both asked for a transfer.

Everything went downhill football-wise for me from that moment.

Towards the end of the 1978/79 season I was out of the team and Brian Kidd was in - signed from Manchester City. I'd played with Brian for the England Under-23s but I didn't get much of an opportunity to team up with him again at Everton. We only took the field a couple of times together but I liked Brian, a guy who continues to have a wonderful career in football to this day as part of Pep Guardiola's coaching set-up at Manchester City.

I have nothing bad to say about the way I departed Everton. Philip Carter was firm but fair. He wasn't going to offer me a better deal, but I liked the way he'd handled the situation. We'd shaken hands and I had gone home to ponder my next move. I'd been very happy at Everton, but it wasn't just Bill Shankly's pep talk about how I should press for a better contract that had niggled me.

We had a guy called Eric Harrison running the reserves. Eric would go on to nurture the youth team at Manchester United that brought through the Neville brothers and David Beckham and the rest of the so-called class of '92. He did an incredible job with those lads and eventually found his niche. Well Eric got promoted to first-team coach, helping Gordon Lee. He filled the void left by Steve Burtenshaw when Steve left to manage my old club QPR. Steve was incredibly popular with the Everton players and Eric had a different style of coaching that didn't go down well. He upset quite a few first-team players, myself included. He was very aggressive and tried to show his authority and had a knack of upsetting people in front of their team-mates. His confrontational style of man-management didn't suit me. I wasn't having that. I felt Eric was out of his depth. The step-up to coaching the first team was too big for him at the time, I felt. So, with that on my mind and the contract dispute also still niggling me, I went to see Gordon Lee and formerly put in a transfer request.

The next thing I know, Gordon informs me that Everton have given me and Bob Latchford permission to speak to Wolves, who had expressed interest in signing both of us.

As a result, Bob and I went to a hotel in the Midlands to meet Wolves boss John Barnwell. As things turned out, Wolves did sign a big centre forward, but it was Andy Gray, not Bob Latchford. Wolves were second in the league and the Andy Gray transfer fee would be a record at that time - £1,469,000. I was about to join a star-studded line-up of signings that would include Willie Carr, Emlyn Hughes and John Richards in addition to Gray.

I'd shaken hands on a pretty good three-year deal with John Barnwell, although after I came home and told Brenda I didn't hear anything from Wolves immediately. The day before I was due to return to Wolves for a second meeting we had a visitor up in Lancashire. It was John Hazell, a guy from Colchester who used to look after all our financial affairs.

I should say at this point that throughout my career I never had an agent. Never felt I needed one. The PFA were aware of what other players earned, so if I picked up the phone and rang Gordon Taylor and asked what he thought was a good wage I should be asking for, Gordon and the PFA would advise you for free. They were good like that. Agents, these days, have become so powerful and influential. Unfortunately, some of the young kids in the game now think they've made it at 17. I do think they are badly guided at times, and I bet their agents aren't in touch with them in 30 years' time. Of course there are some good agents, but some are absolute parasites.

Anyway, John Hazell gave me excellent advice for years on pensions, investments - that sort of thing. So, in the midst of the transfer dealings with Everton and Wolves, I'm at home with Brenda and John when the phone rings at about 11 p.m. The caller was a guy called Jim Greenwood, who was club secretary at Everton.

After apologising for disturbing me so late at night, Jim says: "The choice is yours Dave."

I say, "What choice?" and Jim says, "You can either go to Wolves or Manchester United: United have matched Wolves' offer. Same fee, same wages."

Dave Sexton, who had been such a great manager for me at QPR was now at Old Trafford, managing the biggest club in Britain. And it became apparent that he wanted to work with me again.

Jim said, "I'll leave it to you to decide."

I said "thanks", put the phone down and made my mind up to call the number Jim had given me for the secretary at Manchester United, a guy called Les Olive.

Because I'm a man of my word and I'd shaken on a deal with

John Barnwell, I turned United down. "Much as I admire Dave Sexton and Manchester United Football Club," I found myself saying to Les Olive, "I've decided to go to Wolves."

He wished me all the best in a very professional manner. When I put the phone down, Brenda and John Hazell looked at me astonished. They thought I had rocks in my head!

That night I went to bed thinking about what I had said. I would be a Wolves player with a reported £325,000 price tag round my neck and 5% of that fee in my bank account.

As it turned out, it was the worst decision I ever made. The biggest mistake of my life. Awful. Wolves were in Europe and higher up the league table than United at the time. Was I influenced a little bit by that? Maybe. Was I honourable? Yes, I'd like to think so. Was I stubborn? Almost certainly.

CHAPTER 14

Wolves: The Worst Decision I Ever Made

Most of my time at Wolves I absolutely hated. A very unhappy period in my career. John Barnwell had seemed reasonable enough when I went down to meet him. Born in the north-east, he'd actually played for Bishop Auckland as a young amateur before a distinguished playing career with Arsenal and Nottingham Forest. Wolves were doing okay under his management and I guess at the back of my mind was the fact that, at the time, they were higher in the league and doing rather better than Manchester United, who had come in with an identical offer for me. But things started to unravel quickly once I'd signed for Wolves.

From the outset I never felt comfortable there. I was put up in the beautiful Mount Hotel in Wolverhampton, sharing a room with another new signing, Emlyn Hughes. He was not my favourite room-mate, let's put it that way, and I was missing my family back home.

So, I checked out of there and ended up long-distance commuting to training from my home in the north-west.

The Wolves assistant manager was Richie Barker, the former Shrewsbury Town boss. I hadn't met him when I'd travelled down for talks with John Barnwell. Barker I did not like.

I'd be the first to hold my hand up and say that at Wolves I wasn't performing. I wasn't actually playing much either and had to wait until October for my Wolves debut in a 0-0 draw with Derby. The team were doing okay and there were occasions when you could see the quality that we had in that side. I even managed a 'man of the match' award for my part in a very eye-catching away win - 3-2 at Manchester City in December. I remember it well, because bizarrely I was given a radio and a watch that day to mark the award.

But I struggled with my fitness from day one. I was having a succession of niggling hamstring injuries, which obviously affected my form. I just found it tough to perform regularly at the level I expected. At a players' reunion function a little while back, *Wolverhampton Express & Star* columnist John Lalley reminded me just how frustrating a time it had been for me when he recalled me hitting a screamer into the opposition net from 25 yards at Molineux. There was a collective sigh of relief that at last I had settled down after my move from Everton and things were clicking, only for the goal to be disallowed.

I would go on to make just 15 appearances for Wolves, including four in the club's famous League Cup-winning campaign that season. I also played in the FA Cup for Wolves, but more about that depressing day later.

The medical set-up at Wolves was awful. In my opinion, some

of the staff were unqualified and just not up to the job. Andy Gray had the worst knee ever, but he was desperate to get through the medical and did. Maybe I had been spoilt at QPR and Everton. They had a guy called Richie Roberts at Rangers, but by the time I was at Wolves he'd become physio at Walsall. So, I rang Richie up and asked him to look at me, without Wolves knowing. Being fit enough to play hadn't been a problem in my career up to this point. Now a lot of the time I was sidelined.

Even when I was playing for Wolves it wasn't much fun. Richie Barker and I clashed over my footwear and my preference for not wearing shin pads. As I've said many times, the fact that I wore rubbers rather than studs and had my socks rolled down wasn't a fashion statement. Not an image thing. I just hated shin pads. If Barnwell or Barker had mentioned that as a problem at the outset I might not have signed. They wanted to change me. Almost every day Richie Barker would sarcastically point out to everyone that I'd slipped again in training with my rubbers on. Although it was like a red rag to a bull to me, I never said a word and kept quiet.

Then it all kicked off one day when we played Norwich City in the FA Cup and I gave a goal away. Kevin Bond was behind me ready to pounce and I let the ball run through my legs when I should have cleared it. Well, Richie Barker went for me at half-time in front of everyone. Again I said nothing, but picking my shirt up I chucked it straight in his face.

I was finished. At least I thought I was.

From then on Barker and Barnwell tried to make life so hard for me and told me to train with the reserves and the kids.

Every day I would drive back and forth from the Midlands to Lancashire and I was never once late for training with the reserves.

Although it was a tough period in my life, I did make one very special friend during my time at Wolves. Striker Norman Bell was fantastic. On the odd occasion I would get back late from a game, Norman and his wife Sue used to put me up for the night to save me driving back home to Lancashire. Norman was a Sunderland lad who played quite a few games at centre forward during my time at Wolves.

Don't get me wrong, I got on fine with most of the other Wolves lads and the team were doing pretty well, with or without me. It's just that Norman and Sue went out of their way to help me during my exile from the first team.

Determined to not let the situation at Wolves get me down, I kept my nose clean and did what I was expected to do. Barker and Barnwell did everything to break me. I played for the reserves one day and they made me drive all the way down from the north-west to get on the team coach that was leaving to head for the north-west for a game against Liverpool. They had a guy who was a friend of Richie Barker called Dennis Wilshaw, who was an ex-Wolves player and sports psychologist who they wanted me to see, but I wasn't having that.

Wolves got to the League Cup final that spring and Barnwell and Barker seemingly tried to get me to play in a game against Aston Villa during the week before the Wembley date. The idea was that Wolves were going to play a shadow team to protect those likely to play in the final.

But Barker thought he had found the perfect way to belittle me. Somehow, he had retrieved my boots in their plastic bag out of the skip, where they had been dumped at the training ground, and with everyone present handed them to me and said, "There you are" and "...you're not playing!"

I got in my car and drove off.

The background to all of this was that Brenda had gone out

to buy a new dress for the final. Also, as a squad member, I was being fitted for a new club suit.

Wolves beat Nottingham Forest to win the League Cup, but we didn't get to go to Wembley. I'd had a massive fall-out with Barker and thrown my toys out of the pram! So, we didn't share in all the fun surrounding a Wembley final. People still ask me, "Where is your League Cup winners' medal?" I didn't get one of those either. I probably didn't deserve one, although I had played in a few of the games that had taken us to Wembley, including the away leg of the semi-final against Swindon Town.

Amazingly, I did play one more time for the first team at Wolves a couple of months into the next season. It was a European tie away at PSV Eindhoven. I had a decent enough game and even won 'man of the match' again, but we lost 3-1 and that was me really finished.

When a team halfway around the world came in for me, I jumped at the chance to get as far away from the Wolves coaching staff as possible.

CHAPTER 15

Leaving the "Land of Robots" for Canada

'Thomas Quitting Land of Robots!' was the headline in the *Sunday People*. It might have been a bit sensational, but it pretty much summed up my feeling about English football's increasing reliance on over-coaching players back in 1980. I'd known how to play the game when I'd arrived at Wolves. "Wingers are supposed to provide excitement. Who wants to pay to watch a robot ordered to do a specific job," I was quoted as saying. I was 30 years old and had had a bellyful of coaches and systems in England.

And so I signed for the Vancouver Whitecaps in the North American Soccer League. The contract was for a three-year deal and, no question, going to Canada proved to be an amazing experience.

The set-up they had at the football club was a little odd to say the least. The president was Tony Waiters, who I knew from my Burnley days. Tony had been a cracking goalkeeper for Blackpool

143

and England, and I'd played with him at Turf Moor for a spell. Before I'd signed for the Vancouver Whitecaps, Tony and the club's finance guy Peter Bridgwater had come over to meet me in the UK at a hotel in the Midlands. Both Whitecaps and Wolves had agreed a fee, but as I was arriving for the negotiations on my contract, it wasn't the only deal Waiters and Bridgwater were finalising. At the hotel that day was Vancouver Whitecaps goalkeeper Bruce Grobbelaar and Liverpool manager Bob Paisley. As I was moving from Wolves to Whitecaps, Bruce was going in the other direction - to Anfield.

The day I signed for the Whitecaps I was uneasy about the way the transaction was handled. Obviously, Wolves boss John Barnwell and I definitely hadn't seen eye to eye during my time at Molineux, but I sensed that Whitecaps representative Peter Bridgwater wasn't exactly someone I felt I would end up being pals with.

Anyway, Barnwell, Bridgwater, Brenda and I concluded our meeting and with my signature subsequently on the paperwork I was Canada-bound.

The Vancouver Whitecaps contract clauses were unusual. I'd been advised to have three of those clauses removed, which the club agreed to. Thankfully, I was lucky enough to have Brenda's uncle, Jack Ditchburn, vet the contract. Jack was vice chairman of Sunderland Football Club and a solicitor. His advice would prove to be very useful indeed.

Part of the problem with those contract clauses was that it appeared that in the North American Soccer League you could be transferred without the player having any say in the matter. You could turn up for training one day and be told that you have been sold to Dallas or some other team in America. Remember Colin Boulton, the Derby County goalkeeper? It happened to him.

Colin went in one morning and they told him they'd transferred him.

Another mind-blowing clause was the one where if they determined that you had insufficient skill they could terminate your contract!

Worse still, as far as I was concerned, was the fact that after the April to September outdoor season there was an indoor league you were expected to play in. I very quickly got that clause and the other two deleted from my deal.

The extra winter indoor season wasn't something I wanted to commit to. Fifty-two weeks playing football non-stop, all year round, would have been crippling, although of course a great revenue-earner for the club.

So basically, they couldn't sack me if I wasn't skilful enough, they couldn't transfer me without me having a say in the matter, and they couldn't force me to play in the indoor league.

With the contract sorted out I was ready to begin my new career in Canada. From day one I was pleasantly surprised by how very professional the football club was and they were very generous to begin with. At their expense, the club would fly out mum and dad and my brother to visit us. No question, they took good care of us. And there were some familiar faces already signed to the club. Our Vancouver Whitecaps manager was former Leeds United midfield general Johnny Giles, and during my time at the club we had Peter Lorimer, Terry Yorath, David Harvey, Ray Hankin, Alan Taylor and a young kid called Peter Beardsley playing for us.

No doubt organised through Johnny Giles' Irish connections, my first games for the Vancouver Whitecaps were in pre-season based in Dublin. We beat a University of Dublin side and drew with Athlone Town before heading to England, where we thrashed Wycombe Wanderers, before two defeats at Watford and Sheffield Wednesday.

I liked 'Gilesy'. He could be quietly ruthless - a trait I remembered from his playing days - but he was always honest and straight with me: a refreshing change from my time at Wolves. I quickly got to know my team-mates and then we flew to Canada for the start of the new season, which kicked off in the spring. I say "we", but Brenda, Helen and Polly stayed at home in Lancashire initially. For a time I was on my own in a new country and a new city.

The training and playing regime were very similar to what I'd been used to in England. Johnny Giles could be quite a laid-back character, and one of his trademarks as a coach was his insistence that we got a lot of rest. Johnny was a massive believer in the body recovering properly. You'd get into training about ten o'clock, finish at twelve and then spend the rest of your day with the family, apart from when we were playing away, long distance.

Although afternoons were for recovery, one afternoon me and two other lads went down town to Vancouver city centre for a bit of shopping. The next thing I knew there were police officers shouting at us. No idea where they'd come from. It was quite a scary situation.

We hadn't a clue, but apparently jaywalking was a massive offence over there. We'd crossed on the red light and - no word of a lie - those cops pinned the three of us up against the nearest wall. We had to pay a fine on the spot. They wanted thirty or forty dollars. Typical me, I say: "I'm not paying that!"

Looking back, I'm not sure how but I managed to get the amount of the fine down to $15. One of the officers pocketed the cash and we went on our way. No one had warned us. All three of us went into training the next morning and everyone confirmed we'd been totally in the wrong. Pity they hadn't mentioned it before!

Initially, while I was still waiting for Brenda and the girls to fly over and join me, I told the football club that I didn't want to stay in a hotel and asked if there was any chance of me staying in digs. This they did, and they put me with an amazing family called the Mazzuccos. Mum Sharon and dad Ralph would have been in their late forties or early fifties and they had four boys. Mr and Mrs Mazzucco looked after me as if I was their fifth son. They were an incredible family and Brenda and I are still in touch with them today.

By the time Brenda, Helen and Polly were ready to come out to join me I had found a nice three-storey town house to rent in Vancouver. As our intention was to move as a family to Canada, we put our house back home in Lancashire on the market and waited for offers.

As soon as all four of us were together in Vancouver I got a phone call at the club with some bad news, which forced us all to get on a flight back to England. The call was from Brenda's uncle to tell us the sad news that Brenda's father had passed away. So, we all went back to Sunderland for the funeral.

When life had settled down again and I began playing football, I quickly realised the North American Soccer League was booming. Those were the days of the New York Cosmos with stars like Pelé, and even at Vancouver we'd get crowds of 30,000. Sadly, I was out there after Pelé had finished playing for the Cosmos, so I never got to play against him or the likes of Beckenbauer, or any of those legends.

It was interesting how the passion for football in North America was quite regional. The games didn't attract huge crowds everywhere. I remember playing in front of only a couple of thousand in California. And the match-day rituals were so different out there. Goals were celebrated by cheesy organ music or, in the case of the Portland Timbers, a guy would chain-saw a section of tree to mark the ball hitting the back of the net! It was Mickey Mouse stuff compared to what we were used to in England.

If you were struggling to make ends meet in Britain in the early '80s, living in Vancouver would feel like a millionaire's lifestyle by comparison. Fuel was so cheap and housing was very affordable before the property market out there boomed. There were a lot of British footballers making their way over to try their luck in the NASL. The best example was a lad called Carl Valentine. Carl never quite made the grade in England, but he was the big hero in Vancouver. Another was a lad who had been at Wolves, Les Wilson. They'd have such wonderful lifestyles that they never came back.

It might all sound very glamorous, but there was a big drawback: the travelling. Away games involved playing in Florida one week and New York the next, then on to Minnesota. The resulting time changes made all this pretty tiring. Sometimes we'd be 'on the road' for two weeks at a time. And there was no such thing as a Vancouver Whitecaps team bus. The club would order a fleet of cars for the players at the airports. There were times when this became a real advantage. We were playing Calgary one day and the match got postponed. Considering our situation, I said, "I don't mind driving, so do any of you lads fancy going up to the Rockies?" There were about four of us and we had a day to spare, so I drove us up to Banff and it was wonderful. Great to experience places like that.

Life wasn't as much fun on the pitch! The AstroTurf playing

surfaces didn't help. Unlike the artificial pitches today, it was literally like playing football on a carpet laid on concrete. I couldn't get used to it at all. I'd be racing down the wing, having knocked the ball past the full-back, and run it out of play. The ball would roll much, much quicker than I could catch it. As a result, the style of football that was played in the NASL was more into feet rather than space, which wasn't much good for my game. I tried to adjust, and we did have a good side and a good manager, but I was still suffering from niggling injuries. That season I did manage to turn out 16 times, scoring twice, but I wasn't playing to my full potential.

Domestically, Vancouver was so different. Our girls had been very fortunate when we'd lived in Lancashire. Schooling for Helen and Polly had started just after their fourth birthdays and there were only 20 or so children in the village school in Parbold. In Canada, we noticed some big differences educationally. As a teacher Brenda wasn't impressed. To us, the Vancouver kids seemed a lot more advanced in some ways. Even at a very young age they seemed to have their own door keys, but from an educational point of view our two girls seemed to be going backwards. It was a different culture with a lot of freedom - we were actually quite shocked how different. But we definitely made the most of the opportunity my contract had given us. In our free time, as a family, we enjoyed long drives up to the lakes and mountains. The scenery and the climate were good, and it was a beautiful and healthy environment for Helen and Polly to grow up in.

Then the big crunch came. We'd put our house on the market in Lancashire and done all our homework about shipping the furniture out to Canada. We were close to ending our rental contract and buying a property in Vancouver. At that time there was massive popularity in moving to the west coast of Canada and our stay over there coincided with the start of a boom. House prices were trebling. If we'd managed to sell our house in Lancashire quickly we might have been living in Canada now. As luck would have it, we didn't.

I went back to Lancashire at the end of the NASL season and, as expected, the pay cheques kept coming through.

Because it was the NASL close season I immediately rang up Howard Kendall, who was manager at my old club Everton. I asked Howard if he'd mind me going in to train with Everton that autumn and he said no problem. So, I joined the lads at Bellefield and kept myself fit.

Shortly before returning to England, like the rest of the football world, I was saddened to hear the news that Bill Shankly had died.

Apparently, on the day the news was announced training was cancelled at both Liverpool and Everton. Of course, the memories of my chats with Bill came flooding back. As Kevin Keegan recalled in his autobiography *My Life in Football*, both Merseyside clubs played a part in Bill's incredible years in the area. Kevin was walking beside Bill's coffin on the way to the funeral in West Derby when the cortége turned the corner at Bill's home to pass Everton's Bellefield training complex. Outside, heads bowed, still in their muddy kits, the Everton players lined up to pay their respects.

I hadn't been back in England long when the phone rang and I took a call from Tony Waiters in Canada. His tone was strangely cautious, but he said he'd like to arrange a meeting with me and one or two others on a trip to England.

I quizzed him: "What's it all about?"

"I'd rather keep it to myself for now," he began. "I'll not say anything over the phone."

I was puzzled but agreed to meet him.

When Tony arrived in England he brought Peter Bridgwater with him to my house. We'd met Bridgwater before when we'd agreed the deal that transferred me from Wolves. Brenda didn't care for Bridgwater and I didn't much either. He was an ex-CID man turned finance director of sorts for the Vancouver Whitecaps.

All four of us sat down to talk and Tony dropped the bombshell. "David," he said, "we are going to have to terminate your contract and give you a free transfer."

"What do you mean?" I said, stunned. "Are you serious?"

Immediately, my thoughts were, 'I'm 32, I've got my house up for sale and a wife and two children.'

"Well, the club's struggling and the finances aren't good," Tony replied.

Six months earlier they'd been explaining how fantastic Vancouver was and selling the football club to me - now they were in a mess and trying to offload me and another couple of English lads as their squad was top-heavy with us foreigners.

All I could do was tell them in no uncertain terms that I would be putting the matter in the hands of my solicitor.

Later, it became evident that the club had given all their foreign players three-year contracts, but we were only playing for six months each year. For the other six months they'd stitched themselves up, as us foreign players could sit on our backsides and do nothing but draw our wages during the indoor soccer league season.

Before they left there was an attempt by Waiters and Bridgwater to get me to return to Canada and play in their indoor league, but I wasn't having it.

I said, "I'm sorry Tony, I've known you as a player and now as the president of the Vancouver Whitecaps, but all you need to do is check my contract."

They knew what my contract said, and they couldn't make me go back to Canada, so as you can imagine they weren't very happy. Not happy at all.

So, off the two of them went and I just sat tight. And it got quite nasty in the end. I wasn't going to stop the payments coming into my bank account just because they had made an error in the contract. We were indebted to Brenda's uncle. Jack Ditchburn had done us proud. Peter Bridgwater actually threatened to take us to court in Vancouver in a phone call when I was up at Jack's home in Sunderland. Bridgwater kept skirting round the fact that my contract was watertight and gave us all the spiel about Canadian law and rules.

But Jack could be both ruthless and cool and responded, "Ah - very good! I'm quite happy to come out and go through the Canadian law. I've never been to Vancouver. I look forward to a trip over there!"

Bridgwater knew he was out of his depth. He was dealing with a very shrewd lawyer. Jack's parting jovial remark was, "If you want us to come, you let us know and we'll be there."

After that, there was a deadly hush on the other end of the line.

Waiters and Bridgwater didn't have a leg to stand on.

And the outcome? We came to a financial agreement eventually, thanks to Jack, and never set foot in Vancouver again. Sad in some ways as Brenda and I had, on many occasions, talked about living there permanently.

Whatever the situation with my contract and my fall-out with the Vancouver Whitecaps, if our home in Lancashire had been snapped up by a buyer quickly, we might have been Canadian citizens now.

Coming after the Wolves disaster, it was another football transfer that hadn't worked out. As a family we had loved our time in Vancouver, but as far as my football career was concerned, I'd lost all faith in the people running football clubs.

CHAPTER 16

Boro and Pompey

Following the settlement on my contract with the Vancouver Whitecaps, back home in Lancashire I got a phone call and an offer from Middlesbrough Football Club.

I quite fancied the idea. It was only a short-term deal, but it would mean going back to the north-east, which appealed to me. Actually, there were strong indications that Boro, who were in the top league back then, would offer me a two-year deal when the season ended.

Although I only played for them for a couple of months, I really enjoyed myself. Being back in the north-east meant I could see all my family regularly and stay with mum and dad in West Auckland from time to time.

Ex-Celtic player Bobby Murdoch was the Boro manager. Bobby was a good guy and we got on well, and he had former Spurs full-back Cyril Knowles as his coach, who was also a man I got on with.

To me, it was like a breath of fresh air being at Boro. Even though I was playing in a struggling side, I'd got my mojo back and I was pretty happy with my form once I got going. I made my debut in a goalless draw with Manchester City at Ayresome Park in March, and my regular appearances in such a short space of time was in stark contrast to the lack of games during my spells at Wolves and the Vancouver Whitecaps. I even managed a goal in a 3-1 defeat to Bobby Robson's Ipswich and was fit enough to play every game until the end of the season.

Despite playing in all those 13 games until the end of the season and only being on the losing side in three of them, Boro were relegated.

My short time with them ended, as it had begun, with a 0-0 home draw against the newly crowned league champions, Liverpool.

A month into my time at Boro I'd sensed the club were struggling pretty badly financially. I got a call from the secretary, who said: "Dave, I'm sorry that we can't offer you the two-year contract we talked about. Unfortunately we can only offer you one year."

That left me with a decision to make as I'd already had an offer from my former QPR coach Bobby Campbell, who was now Portsmouth boss.

When Bobby Campbell rang me with the offer of a two-year contract, Brenda and I went down to Chichester to talk to him and we decided to accept the Portsmouth deal. Portsmouth were a mid-table Third Division [now League 1] club back in 1982, but Bobby convinced me that the team he was building were heading in the right direction. I'd got on well with Bobby when he and Gordon Jago were at QPR. And I had no problem moving to the south coast: the area looked beautiful, but moving house was our biggest stumbling block.

The transfer to Portsmouth would be the start of a wonderful 29 years down on the south coast, but first we had to sell our family home in Lancashire.

That was easier said than done. At the back of the property lived a farmer, Gerald Holding. Gerald was a pig farmer, and after we had bought our house he had extended the piggery. As you can imagine, when the wind was in the wrong direction the smell could be horrendous. People in the village complained when his building extensions were first proposed, but nevertheless he got planning permission.

This became a problem. How were we ever going to sell our house?

When I met John Deacon, the chairman of Portsmouth Football Club, I mentioned our difficulty in selling a property that had been on the market for two years without a sale. John was a very wealthy guy and, as luck would have it, he was in the building trade. I had an idea and told John that I'd agree to come down to Portsmouth if he bought the house from us. "If you buy my house and give me what I'm asking for it, I'll sign for Portsmouth," I said.

Obviously, John Deacon had never seen the house but said, "No problem."

He had a son in Carlisle, and en route from a journey north to south, him and his wife called in at our house to view it. He loved the house, but after a good look round I asked him, "What about the pig farm?"

He needn't have worried: after signing for the club I moved to Portsmouth and we'd only been renting a house for five minutes down there when we had a phone call from the estate agents, Ball & Percival, up north.

"Mr Thomas, we've had an offer on your house from two doctors."

I responded by telling them, "I've already got the football club to agree to buy the house." But the estate agent says, "Well, these two doctors have said they can move quite quickly."

So, as it turned out, the football club never had to pay for it!

The two doctors bought it and they're still there now, although the piggery is long gone. Sadly, the place is an absolute tip these days. It breaks my heart when I go back up there.

I played 30 league games for Portsmouth over a couple of seasons. As had happened before, I didn't exactly hit the ground running at my new club. I was in plaster for the first three months of the 1982/83 season following an Achilles tendon injury. Then I started getting hamstring pulls. I wasn't playing as well as I knew I could and it was one niggling injury after another. After a while, a lad called Alan Rogers took my place. Alan was an ex-Plymouth Argyle winger and he did exceptionally well when he came in. There were no hard feelings on my part towards Alan or Bobby Campbell.

Bobby had been right to talk up Portsmouth. We won the old Third Division title in that first season and I got a winner's medal. Crucially, Bobby Campbell signed Mark Hateley. Another big, tall centre forward I rated. Very good young player. Mark scored 22 league goals that season, with Alan Rogers or me supplying the crosses. He did so well he was sold to Italian giants AC Milan at the end of the season.

The running of the club was a bit unprofessional and chaotic at times. Les Allen was the commercial manager and the club were sponsored by a kit company called Le Coq Sportif. All the stock went to Bobby Campbell's house for him to distribute! Fratton Park and the club's facilities were rather antiquated compared to what I'd been used to. And the playing staff were split into two camps. There had been a big influx of new players when I joined. They signed Ernie Howe, Alan Biley and Neil Webb, and all of us were on bigger salaries than the players already at the club. No real surprise there. Where the club made a mistake was in giving each one of us a brand-new Toyota car. Understandably, I think that led to some jealousy among the senior pros who had been there a while.

Through no fault of his own, Ernie Howe wasn't a great signing for the club. He is, to this day, one of my very best friends, but his career ended almost as soon as it had begun at Portsmouth. In a game at Fratton Park, Ernie was playing, solid as ever, at centre back when his own team-mate Mick Tait missed the ball in the penalty box and kicked Ernie on the kneecap. The physio came on to treat Ernie and he tried to continue, but he suffered a bad fracture that sadly led to him retiring from football. He was devastated. Although lost to professional football, Ernie ended up working with his brother-in-law in the building trade and managed Basingstoke Town FC for a number of years.

Bobby Campbell's initial success at Pompey wasn't sustained after promotion, and when we finished in the bottom half of the league Bobby was sacked.

In May 1984, Alan Ball was appointed manager.

Although I'd played with him at international level and respected him as a World Cup winner, he and I were total opposite characters. 'Bally' was a bit like Marmite. You either liked him or you didn't. He loved a drink and a gamble on the horses, just as a lot of players did back then. He'd always treated me okay up to a point, but I felt he was a bit of a loose cannon.

While I still had a contract as a player, John Deacon told 'Bally' that he'd like to appoint me as youth team coach. I don't think 'Bally' had much say in the matter. He would manage the first team and I would look after the reserves and the youth team. After a difficult pre-season with 'Bally' not exactly setting the right example as manager of Portsmouth Football Club, my respect for him wasn't high. I never really felt part of the coaching set-up.

New managers always bring their own men in with them if they can. To be fair, 'Bally' did try to help me, but I found it hard. There was the whole school of excellence thing to contend with and it was pretty gruelling work. I was still playing while coaching and supervising night matches and weekend games for the reserves and youth sides. Don't get me wrong - I really enjoyed coaching the youngsters because they all wanted to learn. But overall the workload was a real killer.

'Bally' had the idea to bring Graham Paddon in to help with the workload. He and Graham had played together in Hong Kong and were massive drinking buddies, and the decision was made for Graham to take the reserves and me to concentrate on the youth teams. That suited me, not least because the reserve team manager's job is a thankless task. You get to work with the players who aren't playing in the first team, and they're all moaning and groaning because they've been dropped. Win, lose or draw, it didn't really matter to them in reserve games. But the youth team was different. Perhaps I was drawing on my experiences of winning the FA Youth Cup with Burnley. But I loved that part of my job.

The first team were doing well under 'Bally'. Portsmouth

were in the running for promotion to the top division but we missed out, only on goal difference, to third-place Manchester City, who went up with Oxford United and Birmingham City. A dramatic last match of the season saw Pompey win 2-0 at Huddersfield Town, but it was not quite enough. My playing contract was coming to an end and I played my last game for Portsmouth during that run-in. Saturday the 20th of April 1985 at Selhurst Park turned out to be my last game in league football. We lost 2-1 to Crystal Palace, which handed the initiative to a Manchester City side that beat us by the same score at Fratton Park a week later.

So, at the end of the season, 'Bally' tells me, "The chairman wants to see you and I don't think it's good news. I don't think he's going to offer you another contract."

I was okay with that. There had to be cutbacks - I understood that. Fair enough. At 34 I was going to have to retire, but I knew financially I could manage. 'Bally' had suggested after the final game of the season that he was proud of his young side and I clearly wasn't getting any younger. And if 'Bally' and Graham could handle the first team, reserves and youth coaching between them then good luck to them.

Anyway, as expected John Deacon called me in and said, "I'm sorry to say we won't be renewing your contract, Dave, and we are just going to go with Alan and Graham running the first team, reserves and youth team."

He went on to echo what 'Bally' had told me about the financial restrictions behind the move.

We shook hands and I thanked him for giving me the opportunity and we wished each other all the best.

I wasn't prepared for what happened next.

There was a phone call two weeks later from a guy called Mike

Neasom, who was the sports editor for the local Portsmouth newspaper, *The News*.

"Have you heard what's happened Dave?" said Mike. "Peter Osgood has just taken over as youth team coach."

I couldn't believe it.

'Bally' had set it all up behind my back.

I thought, 'the sneaky so and so'. If he'd told me that was his plan and he was bringing his mate in I would have been fine with it. But it was the way the whole thing was done that really angered me.

How much did I want to turn my back on football at that time? Well, I'd had enough. My response to a kind job offer a few days later gives you some idea how upset I was. And that approach was from someone I respected. The phone rang, and on the line was Bruce Rioch, who'd taken over as boss at Middlesbrough. I'd played with Bruce at Everton and he was one of the good guys.

Bruce was great. "Sorry to hear you've lost your job at Portsmouth, but I'd like to offer you the job of reserve team coach up here at Middlesbrough."

It was a decent offer too, but my immediate response was an emotional one: "No thanks. You could offer me the first-team coach job Bruce, but I'd still want nothing to do with it! Thanks, but I'm finished with football."

Since leaving Everton I'd encountered the worst in football people. I was more and more disillusioned and angry. The men I worked for in the early years of my career were straight-down-the-line honest people. But the fall-out from my spells at Wolves and Portsmouth had hurt like hell.

CHAPTER 17

What Am I Going to do Now?

People talk about footballers retiring in their thirties. I was 34 when I finished at Pompey, but although I was finished with professional football I wasn't finished with the game completely. Admittedly, I was out of love with the game at the highest level, but I've always kept in touch with the great friends I made at all the clubs I played for. I would even get the chance to get involved at non-league level and later go back to Pompey to do some radio work. When the end came in May 1985, I wasn't going to put my feet up.

Immediately after turning down the reserve team coaching job at Middlesbrough, it dawned on me: what am I going to do now?

As a family, we were lucky. There were no immediate financial worries, so I wasn't too concerned about where the money was coming from. We were settled down in West Sussex. The village of Prinsted, where we lived, was a beautiful spot and our girls were happy at school and with years of secondary education ahead of them.

I wasn't an avid golfer, although I joined Cowdray Park Golf Club at Midhurst, and Goodwood Golf Club. To begin with, for a few days, I didn't have a clue how I would fill my time that summer. I didn't fancy running a pub, like so many of my fellow retired footballers seemed to do back then. So, I set up my own gardening business!

For four or five pounds an hour, I was cutting hedges and mowing lawns and weeding borders. Now I was in my element. I'd always been particularly passionate about grass and vegetables; I'd got that interest from my dad. In the great north-east tradition, he used to grow some massive leeks and I would watch him keenly as a boy. My gardening bug had never gone away. My business grew and grew, and I absolutely loved it. I was lucky in that I didn't have to rely on it for my income as my football pension was pretty good and Brenda was an experienced art and technology teacher, head of department, and out all day. So, I'd set off gardening every morning in my little Morris Minor van. On my own, no hassle from anybody, and with some wonderful customers.

One of my best clients was a guy called Mr Shand. He'd moved from London to Chichester and he'd just had his garden landscaped. It was beautiful. He didn't know I was a former footballer and I worked for him for the full two years I had my gardening business. When we got to know each other better he asked me if I wanted help paying for the van that I needed for my business! He was concerned I couldn't meet the payments and offered to loan me the money. I told him it wasn't a problem, but he was lovely like that. And when he discovered I was mad keen on fishing he enabled me to fish the River Test, which is just about the best dry fly trout river in the world. It turned out that for most of his working life Mr Shand had the rights to fish a stretch on the Test. We got chatting over a cup of tea one day and my eyes lit up when he said, "David, would you like to come fishing with me one day?"

Well you can imagine how I felt. True to his word he took me down to the Test and showed me where to fish. I couldn't believe my luck. Second cast I got into a 4-lb brown trout!

Sadly, Mr Shand passed away when I was on holiday in Menorca. I was quite upset when I got the news. He was such a wonderful man and he'd always been very good to me. When I returned from holiday I went round to his house to pay my respects and his wife opened the door and invited me in.

"David," she said, "would you like Mr Shand's fishing beat?"

I nearly fell over. Those beats on the Test don't come up very often for resale so I jumped at the chance to take it on and fished that stretch of river near a village called Stockbridge every Thursday for 20 years. My record during all that time was a 6-lb 12-oz brown trout.

During my gardening years I was asked by Jack Pearce, manager at Bognor Regis Town Football Club, if I'd play and coach the team. I was pretty raw about what had happened at Portsmouth so I went away to think about it and had a meeting to get to know Jack before saying 'yes'. Jack was great and will always be a life-long friend. He trusted me, I trusted him, and I loved my time there. I played for a year and was coach for five more years, when I'd take training on Tuesday and Thursday nights. The Bognor players were a great bunch of lads to work with. No confrontations and a pleasure to coach. It helped restore my love of football. We got to the first round of the FA Cup three seasons running in the mid-to-late '80s, even getting as far as

Round 2 in 1985. In one of those cup games we played Torquay United. They were managed at the time by the ex-Spurs full-back Cyril Knowles, who, coincidentally, had been my coach when I'd played for Middlesbrough a couple of years previously.

When I finished at Bognor that really was the end of my playing and coaching career as I hadn't the time I needed to devote to it once I began a new PE teaching role. Those were six very happy years I spent at Bognor.

Although football began to play a less important role in my life, I never completely turned my back on it. Occasionally, through my contacts in the game, I'd get invited to matches here and there. Probably the most dramatic game I witnessed as a spectator was at Anfield on the 26th of May 1989. Every Liverpool and Arsenal fan will know what I'm referring to. Both clubs had been battling it out to win the league and Arsenal needed to beat the home side by two clear goals to take the title. The fixture had been put back to the end of the season. The original date had been just a week after Liverpool's traumatic FA Cup semi-final against Nottingham Forest which had resulted in the Hillsborough disaster, when 96 Liverpool fans lost their lives. This Liverpool versus Arsenal game turned out to be a game to savour, and my Bognor Regis Town friend Jack Pearce wanted to go. Jack loved the way Liverpool played at the time. Happily, Liverpool boss Kenny Dalglish very kindly got Jack and I tickets for the game. Jack's love for Liverpool extended beyond that of an ordinary fan. His dream had always been to go on to the pitch at Anfield, even in the empty stadium, and kick a ball into the net at the Kop end. Anyway, we took our seats for a match that ended, as most football fans will know, with Michael Thomas scoring a late goal in added time to see Arsenal run out 2-0 winners and pinch the title from Liverpool. My big memory that night was at 0-1 when

Liverpool's John Barnes, instead of keeping the ball in the corner to run the clock down, tried to cross the ball into the penalty area. Kenny Dalglish never forgave John for that! With time running out, the ball ended up in the hands of Arsenal goalkeeper John Lukic. Lukic then threw the ball to Lee Dixon, who hit a 40-yard pass to Michael Thomas, who got on the end of it and scored. Jack and I went downstairs after the game and Kenny asked us into his office. You could have cut the atmosphere with a knife! Sadly, Jack never got his dream walk out on to the pitch. If Liverpool had won the league that night, Jack could have taken a hundred balls and kicked them on the hallowed turf.

These days, Jack sits on the FA Council and we still chat on the phone from time to time.

When my gardening business was really taking off, an ex-marine called Roger Gilliat called me up. Roger worked in the PE department at the school my girls attended as pupils and asked me if I was interested in doing some football coaching. I happily agreed and I did that twice a week. Then the school, Bishop Luffa School in Chichester, offered me a part-time job on the staff.

No qualifications, no degree, no A- or O-Levels. Brenda said when she saw the application form, "How are you going to fill that in?"

I think I signed what amounted to mostly blank sheets of paper and sent it back to Chichester's education department, and blow me they accepted me!

So, I left my gardening business and became a part-time teacher, and astonishingly went on to do that job for 20 happy years. I think I learnt just as much as the students. Any sports course they offered me, on say athletics or cricket, I used to go on.

My new part-time career had obviously attracted the attention of the football world. I was invited to be filmed for a new TV show. I had the great fortune to be the subject of one of football commentator and presenter Brian Moore's last interviews before he died. He came to Bishop Luffa School with a film crew to do one of those 'where are they now?' type of programmes. We filmed it in the sports hall, much to the amusement of some of my pupils, who called out witty comments from the balcony above. And Brian was great. Exactly the gentleman you saw on TV.

The best thing I remember about my time as a teacher was the staff in that PE department. The most genuine people I have ever worked with. I found something that was a complete contrast to my last days in football. Honest people I could trust.

I don't want you to get the impression I was trying to push football out of my life. I still enjoyed watching as opposed to playing the game. It's just that I was enjoying new experiences and meeting some lovely people. But then came an opportunity to enjoy football in a completely new way.

While I was still teaching during the late 1990s, a lovely chap called Peter Hood got in touch with me. Peter was the south of England football commentator for Capital Gold. His boss was a guy called James Haddock, who is now one of the chief golf reporters for Sky. Peter had a proposition and asked me if I was interested in working as his commentary partner for the broadcasts for all the Portsmouth games. Having never done anything like that before I wasn't sure to begin with, but I decided to give it a go and thoroughly enjoyed my new role. It was a new interest for me and fitted pretty well with my part-time teaching schedule. The commentaries were live broadcasts and we travelled all over the country together covering Pompey games. I had to develop a new knack of engaging my brain before speaking, as the tiniest mistake would obviously be picked up by the listeners. It kept me on my toes, and I hope my contributions never sounded too much like personal criticism. My approach was always to give constructive criticism when players made mistakes. I was once described by Peter as having a commentary style that is "short and to the point", which I think was a compliment! I always tried not to pussyfoot around the incidents that came up in games I covered. I think I was blunt when I needed to be and full of praise when a player deserved it.

When part of Capital radio closed down and formed another company, James Haddock asked me to join him in a new venture, covering Southampton matches. To say I thought this was odd was an understatement. All football fans know how much rivalry there is between the respective Portsmouth and Southampton football clubs. I had no connections with the club up to that point and had never played for them. But I enjoyed the change and found myself on commentary duties for the newly formed Southampton FC radio station called The Saint. My task was to work as co-commentator, with James this time, on all the away matches while Jimmy Case covered the home games. This was during the era when Gordon Strachan was managing the Saints.

Looking back on my days commentating for both clubs, I guess I always felt more connected to Pompey than the Saints, although I've got a lot of time for both clubs. One of the reasons for that was my good friend Mark Trapani. Mark was a life-long Pompey fan and became a director at the club. When owner Milan Mandaric sold out to businessman Alexandre Gaydamak, the club eventually suffered a disastrous period in its history, which was very sad to watch. What I liked about Mark was that when the club hit rock bottom, he got rid of all the hospitality, wining and dining and entertaining at Pompey. Clearly the club were living above their means. They could not afford to pay the wages of the superstars they were bringing in. Jermain Defoe, Sol Campbell, David James, Peter Crouch - the wage bill must have been phenomenal. There was a price to pay for all the success they had, but the fans witnessed some great times with an FA Cup win and European football. Mark and a group of business friends rescued the club and got it debt free. In 2017, the Pompey Supporters' Trust voted in favour of a proposed bid by an American investment company, headed by former Walt Disney Company chairman and chief executive Michael Eisner, to take over the club. Mark is a shrewd businessman, but it had broken his heart to see Pompey in the state it had been in. Just as well he was a workaholic. You wouldn't believe the number of meetings he attended to save that club. I have great admiration for him, and he was the man I picked up the phone to when I wanted to find out about my last game for Portsmouth and last game in league football for this book. I didn't know. Thankfully, and typical of Mark, he did!

Happily, Pompey are on the up again currently and the memories of that terrible saga we all witnessed when the club almost went under are fading fast.

When I wasn't gardening, teaching, fishing or commentating I found a new, very worthwhile hobby. Brenda had always loved horses and was a good rider when she was a girl, so when the opportunity arose to volunteer for the Riding for the Disabled Association Carriage Driving Group at Goodwood, we both offered to help. At the same time, Brenda was learning how to break in a pony with a friend of hers, Kay, who worked for the Duchess of Richmond, who was also heavily involved in the charity.

Although I hadn't considered the practicalities at all, I felt Brenda should have her own pony.

As luck would have it, Hilary Gilson, a neighbour, tipped me off about a pony which I secretly went and bought from a breeder called Alison Clarke. She was a little Welsh Section A pony and Alison and I walked her to our house. At the front door, we attached a big blue ribbon to the pony and I rang the doorbell. When Brenda opened the door I said, "Happy birthday Brenda!"

Well, although she was delighted with Burco, as we called her, her first thoughts were 'What am I going to do with that?!' As it turned out, a plan was hatched to break Burco in to drive with a trap so she could be used for the Riding for the Disabled Association. Not unnaturally, Brenda was also quite keen to find out where we were going to keep her, bearing in mind that at the time we didn't have any land to speak of.

We stabled her to begin with at the place I'd bought her from and, after day after day working with her, we eventually succeeded in breaking her in and Burco made the most fantastic driving partner. We still have her today and she's 14 years old.

CHAPTER 18

"Mr Thomas, Sorry to Inform You..."

In the year 2000 I was 50. Like a lot of people at that age, I felt my eyes were deteriorating to the extent where I felt I needed reading glasses. Off I went to the local optician in Chichester and he checked my field of vision. He completed the tests and then came back and said, "Mr Thomas, we have a problem. There are quite a few dark patches on your fields of vision. We need to refer you to see a specialist."

As a result, the optician wrote out a letter and I went to the King Edward VII Hospital in nearby Midhurst. I was there for a scan. I had an idea what was going on because one of Brenda's aunts found out she had cancer behind the eye, so I knew what they were looking for. I came out, the report went back to the consultant, and although the report was okay and there was no cancer present and I could still drive, he said, "Really you should inform the DVLA."

Actually, as it turned out, the hospital contacted the DVLA

and I informed my insurance company. Meanwhile, I was sent to an independent optician local to me in Emsworth to do another field of vision test. Although I don't think they are supposed to tell you anything, typical cheeky me I asked the optician how she thought I'd done.

The woman got up and gave me the thumbs up and said, "I think you are going to be okay."

More or less at the same time I had a response from the DVLA, which pretty much said, "All good at the moment. We will issue you with a three-year driving licence."

So, I thought great! Thank God. I was still teaching at the time and driving was a vital part of my working life, ferrying school sports teams back and forth.

Three years on and I headed back to the optician in Emsworth for my obligatory field of vision tests. Same question from me: "How do they look?" Same answer from the optician: "Okay, fine."

I was just about to leave to go to school one September morning about two weeks later when the postman brought the mail.

"Your fan mail's here," Brenda joked, as she often did when the post arrived. I'd still get the odd letter from Burnley, QPR or Everton fans or even visits on the doorstep sometimes. Anyway, among the various letters and bills that morning was a brown envelope, which I opened. It looked important. Then I began to scan the contents and called out to Brenda, "Come and have a look at this!" And I read out loud. "Dear Mr Thomas, we are sorry to inform you that you are unable to drive again."

There it was in stark black and white. I could hardly believe what I was reading.

Well, it was a shock. And my first thought was, 'How am I going to get to school?'

I don't think either of us were thinking straight, but after a minute or two Brenda said, "You'll have to catch a bus."

But I was so knocked for six - I took the car. I was so bloody-minded. I shouldn't have, but I did. Absolutely ridiculous what I did.

Turning to Brenda I said, "Well I haven't seen the post this morning" and stormed out of the house.

If I had accidentally hurt someone, or worse still killed anybody, I would have been sent to prison. Awful.

And then I had to tell the school I couldn't take the kids to matches or drive them anywhere. 'What am I going to do? I'm snookered,' I thought. I still desperately wanted to teach while I could still see.

The whole day was spent thinking about that letter and what was about to become a pretty major change in my life.

Naturally I began to think that, surely, I could appeal against the decision. Before proceeding with an appeal, I managed to persuade a consultant to come out to the house to test me.

Sitting in the front of our car, I had our friend GP Sue Logan sit behind me. The consultant went out to the windscreen and got a pen and put it in line with me and I didn't see it until it was right on top of me.

"I know it's a simple test," he said, "but that's it, I'm afraid. It's a waste of time appealing."

I was gutted.

I handled the situation the best way I could. From then on I took the bus to school every day. It was difficult, but I managed to stay positive. My boss Colin and the rest of the staff at school were brilliant.

In sport and life you have highs and lows. I'd had bad form to deal with, criticism, injuries, and I think dealing with the pressure of those problems definitely helped me with my sight loss. Remembering what Dave Sexton had always said, I think I've always been pretty consistent - "I never get low, I never get high" - but I consider myself a happy, positive person. I had to be. Because if you lose your driving licence and your sight and if you rely on a car for your job, the structure of your whole life changes. I was lucky I was in the financial position where I didn't have to work full-time, but if I was on the road as a rep or a businessman, with a family and mortgage - bloody hell, what would I have done? In my case, I always thought there was a solution.

In the summer of 2010 we moved house and, after many happy years on the south coast, bought the home of our dreams.

I always said during my football career that I'd one day return to the north-east to live. Brenda was Sunderland born and bred, our wedding, the girls' christenings, family - all the significant events in our life had been celebrated there. We knew one particular place that would fit the bill if we ever moved back and it wasn't far from where I grew up in County Durham.

In 2000 we had rented a lovely rural property called Dairy Cottage from its owner, a man called John Mayhew, who also owns the famous Rules restaurant in London. The cottage was in a village called Lartington and was only a few miles from my childhood home in West Auckland and where I went to school in Barnard Castle. We brought Brenda's mother, who was in her eighties, to stay with us and she'd look out from her chair and say, "This is heaven." She'd been living locally so it was nice for her to stay there with us after her home had been sold. The place had peacocks and a wonderful garden, and while we were holidaying there Brenda did some wonderful pencil sketches in her diary of

Dairy Cottage. One note she added to the diary read, "I wish one day this could be my home."

After Brenda's mum passed away, we'd still ring up John Mayhew and ask if it was available and we continued renting it quite regularly.

One day Brenda and I were on our way up to Sheffield from the south coast to see my youngest daughter Polly and I had a call from the local gamekeeper up in Lartington, Phil Morgan. He said, "I think John is putting Dairy Cottage on the market."

When we arrived at Polly's we had the opportunity to get on the internet and see if we could find out more. Blow me, it had just come on the market. So instead of going home south we drove north and I spoke to John Mayhew in the garden at Dairy Cottage.

"John," I said, "obviously we haven't sold our own house but we really want to buy Dairy Cottage."

Helpfully, John promised to give us a head start and said, "I'll give you three months to sell your property down south."

Well it was nice of him to do that, but it didn't give us much time. We went away and made him an offer.

Brenda and I returned south and immediately had our house measured up and put up for sale by the agent. On the market it went, and it was sold within four days!

Happily, two buyers wanted it and it was the subject of two sealed bids. We could not believe our luck. We completed in five weeks. It was obviously meant to be! We had the home of our dreams and moved in that summer.

Our new home had once been part of an estate - the walled garden to Lartington Hall. When John Mayhew's aunt, Mrs Olive Field, lived at the hall she owned our current home, which was an area of land that supplied all the fruit and vegetables to the hall. When she died, the Lartington estate passed to John in the 1980s and he converted one side of the old potting shed and old workshop into a cottage - where our conservatory is now was once the estate's huge compost heap! What is now Dairy Cottage was sold off privately and we now have lovely gardens overlooking the hall and stables for the horses and ponies. Apart from looking after the livestock, Brenda still paints. There are examples of her artwork all around our place and she still has a studio on the property. She also continues carriage driving.

Although the withdrawal of my driving licence in 2000 had been a bombshell, in most respects my eyesight hadn't deteriorated too badly since. It wasn't until 2010, when we moved back up north, that I began to realise that I had serious problems.

It was recommended I go to the Royal Victoria Infirmary in Newcastle. Not a place I look back at with good memories. Most visits turned out to be bad experiences. I had three operations on my left eye, which didn't go particularly well, and whenever I had an appointment there I'd feel myself getting really worked up in advance. I felt the treatment wasn't the best and I wasn't comfortable with the consultant I was assigned to. I'd paid to go private - something paid for by the Everton Former Players' Foundation and organised by a guy called Harry Ross, which I was very grateful for. What really upset me was the reaction from the consultant just two weeks after he'd operated on me.

"Have I seen you before?" was his opening line!

I wasn't impressed. Anxious and angry, it felt like there was steam coming out of my ears. Anyway, I left him wanting assurances that if I returned again, as I would be an NHS patient, that I would see him again rather than chop and change with other people. This he agreed.

When I returned next time, I was greeted by a whiteboard

outside the consultation room with his name on it. My relief was short-lived.

Brenda and I took our seats in the waiting room and a woman called me in to the little room where you look at the optician's alphabet cards before you see your consultant. I happened to mention to the woman looking after my test, "I'm glad to see Mr so and so is here today."

She hesitated for a few moments before responding, "No… he's on vacation."

Well, I can tell you, I went absolutely ballistic. I completely lost it.

"He's on vacation?! But his name's on that whiteboard!"

They had to get another eye consultant to come over and calm me down.

"How would you feel," I asked her, "if you came to see this guy as expected and he was on vacation?" The poor woman didn't know what to say. She felt so sorry for me, but there was little she could do.

Having done a fair amount of research ourselves into who could help me in the north-east, all I could do before leaving the RVI for the last time was to ask her to get all my records together and send them to the Sunderland Eye Infirmary.

Angry and frustrated, I just had to hope that the Sunderland Eye Infirmary would give me the treatment I needed.

My first visit there was to see a guy called Mr Fraser. He then operated and solved the problem a little bit, but immediately began to give me confidence that he could help. Every six months I see him. He's calm, knowledgeable and very honest. Everything I need from someone helping me with my deteriorating vision. The treatment is as wonderful as my previous experiences were awful.

CHAPTER 19

'Registered Blind'

My medical records say I'm registered blind/partially sighted. The best way I can describe how I see the world is as a horse with blinkers on. I have no peripheral vision at all. That's completely shot to bits. It's a hereditary problem. I've got severe glaucoma. My father became totally blind, but, thank God, my brother is OK.

I think it was Brenda who first suggested the idea that perhaps we should contact the Guide Dogs charity. In the early days I think my immediate reaction to her was, "A guide dog? I don't need a guide dog!" You go through denial, as they say.

In one of the local villages, Eggleston, there was a lady with a guide dog, or, in this case, what they call a buddy dog - a retired guide dog. She had a condition the opposite to mine where her peripheral vision was good but straight ahead was poor. We got talking and I began to realise that maybe I could qualify for a guide dog.

Although it set me thinking, I did no more until after an awful experience which changed my attitude.

The day in question should have been fun, but it was anything but. During a trip south to visit my daughter Helen, we went to the races at Epsom. It was the week of the Derby and, as you'd expect, it was heaving with people. Then, all of a sudden, I'm thinking, 'There's too many people here for me.' We walked through a tunnel at the course where a race had just finished and people were walking towards us and I just turned to Brenda and said, "Get me out of here."

I couldn't cope. I thought I was going to walk into everyone. I could feel myself getting worked up.

That day, I conceded that Brenda was right. I did need help.

I sat down quietly in a tent with a glass of wine and gathered my thoughts.

For a few weeks afterwards I began to feel quite low. Socially I didn't feel comfortable.

So we contacted The Guide Dogs for the Blind Association and the incredible process began.

They sent a lady called Linda Oliver, along with her partner, to meet me at home. Linda was totally blind. It's easy to remember that meeting. It was a boiling hot day and we sat in the garden of Dairy Cottage. Linda was inspirational. We talked for four hours. There were so many questions. At the end of the interview she had enough information to take back with her to add to medical reports and opinions from my consultants. Before Linda left, she said there were two important things I should remember well. One was that there were no guarantees I would get a guide dog. From the time they are six weeks old to the day they retire, the average cost to train a guide dog is over £55,000. That figure includes training and equipment costs as well as vet fees and dog food, which Guide Dogs offer to pay for throughout a dog's lifetime. She told me there were around 5,000 guide dogs in the UK and all of them had to be specifically trained to be paired with the right person. The charity has to be completely sure that the money is well spent and with the right people.

The second issue was just how important it was for me to understand the need for white-cane training, so that everyone would know my sight was impaired and to increase my mobility and confidence in public, preparing me for a guide dog.

When the time came for me to accept the important support I needed, Linda was one of four people who helped change my life.

Another was Dave Waterfall Brown. Dave became my mobility instructor for the white cane. I learnt so much about that white cane you would not believe. He took me on escalators, we went to crowded places like Darlington, Newcastle and Middlesbrough. Every week for hours and hours. There was so much to take on board. But I was up for it. I wanted to learn everything and I wanted to learn fast.

Two years later - in 2015 - I was contacted by Rachel Manders, a Guide Dogs mobility instructor, who also came out to my home. If I were to have a guide dog there was so much I needed to learn. The first thing Rachel ever did on day one was lead me outside to our drive to test how quickly I walk. This was vital information she needed in pairing me with a dog. I'm a quick walker and there are dogs that walk at a variety of speeds.

Next, she experimented with two different dogs to see how I got on in my local town, Barnard Castle.

Rachel waited until we got back home, then we both sat down. Then came the words I'd hardly dared to expect.

"I'm putting you forward for a guide dog Dave," she said.

That was an emotional moment.

It felt great. By this time I was so positive about the future and how I could cope.

Rachel left me with the news that I was going on the waiting list, but I had no certain idea how long it would take until I was matched up. Understandably, getting a guide dog is a long and carefully planned process.

The fourth and final Guide Dogs for the Blind representative to visit me was Clare Tansley. It was Clare's responsibility to get the right match between me and my dog and for the rural environment in which I lived. Like an invisible undercover agent, she'd send me out on familiar local journeys on my own and follow me to observe where I went and how I moved. This was to judge all my needs and get the perfect guide dog match. How fast did I walk? How did I get on a bus? All those things were noted in readiness for me receiving a guide dog. In her 20 years working for The Guide Dogs for the Blind Association, Clare admitted she'd had just one other blind person, a man from the Lake District, who lived in a similar rural location. My dog wouldn't need to worry so much about footpaths and kerbs. It would have to cope with our livestock - the chickens, geese and ponies we have at home.

Clare sent me to a hotel in Eaglescliffe and I trained with another guy called Dave Adamson, who like me needed a dog. Dave was in a far worse position than me. He and I just hit it off right away. The poor man was so worried who he was going to get as he was a very insecure guy. So I was training with a dog called Hannah and Dave was training with a Black Labrador called Quinn. Dave only had a tiny bit of vision and the first thing he said to me was, "Bloody hell. Why have they given me a black one? I cannot see it! I can see yours!"

Guide Dogs paid for both of us for two weeks in that hotel.

They paid for everything including food, but not drinks. So, I bought the wine one night and Dave would buy it the next. Those costs went on your room bill and then you'd settle up on a Friday.

They had students serving the food in the hotel and I'd invited Dave Waterfall Brown, my cane instructor, over for a meal with us. Both our dogs were under the table and this young kid, instead of taking the wine bill to reception, chooses one of us to sign for the drinks. Well, at a pinch I could have just about signed if I had to, but the lad went towards Dave and said, "Mr Adamson, can you sign for the drinks please."

Dave, who was a bit of a comedian, said, "Sign for the fucking drinks?! Can't you see we've got a couple of guide dogs here?" The poor lad - all he could do was back away and apologise, but Dave, Dave and Dave all erupted in hysterics.

CHAPTER 20
Hannah and Me

Most people would think to be a guide-dog owner you would have to be totally blind. That's not the case now. But they don't give dogs away lightly. Now I have Hannah, it's some comfort to know that if I do go 100% blind I will always have a guide dog until the day I die.

Hannah is a Golden Labrador and was just two years old when I got matched with her. She and I bonded immediately.

She's very lady-like. People have noticed and commented on the fact that when she lies down she crosses her front legs. Quite unusual apparently. Not surprisingly, she's the most playful and loveable dog I've ever had. We had a Black Labrador bitch as a pet before and she was lovely, but Hannah is so well trained and connected to me. Once you put her in work mode - once the harness goes on - you could put a tank next to her and she wouldn't bat an eyelid. But what's great is that when she's not working she's like any normal dog. And if she can get on the kitchen worktop and nick some food she will do. There's more than a little bit of naughtiness about her. But I like that.

And she is great around other dogs. She likes to play with them and there is never any sign of aggression at all.

With a guide dog, what I found out very early on is that it's all about routine. When she goes out to do her business every morning she'll almost talk rather than bark to let me know she wants to go outside. It's uncanny. Then I'll feed her and then we'll go off for a walk, whatever the weather, and we do get some extreme weather up here.

She sleeps next to me in her bed, and although she's very good with Brenda it's noticeable that she is my dog. If I get up to go to the loo in the middle of the night Hannah will get up and follow me. If Brenda gets up, she'll maybe look up but stay put next to me.

Outside of the home environment, it's still all about routine. Our first trip out together was practised many times before I went out solo, so to speak, with Hannah. My two most obvious excursions would be to the local bus stop and to the nearby village of Cotherstone. Clare Tansley from Guide Dogs would come with me at first, but when Hannah and I made our first visit to my local town alone we were so well practised I actually felt quite confident. My trust in Hannah, by this time, was complete.

Regular activity is important. You have to be disciplined enough to keep doing what you are doing. If the weather is awful you've still got to venture out together. If I were blind and living on my own and didn't take Hannah out, the routine would collapse immediately. A dog not working regularly can easily lose all the training they've been given.

In my case, I'll get out every day. When we are on the move

I'll be talking to Hannah constantly. Encouraging her to find the kerb and take me here and there. And every Monday I can go into Barnard Castle on the bus, get off the bus, cross the road, and Hannah will take me straight into Clarendon's cafe for coffee and cake.

Further afield, my first long-distance journey with Hannah was to Birmingham. I nearly turned it down. I was invited by Guide Dogs to do a talk at their annual awards presentation event in front of 200 people. Eventually I committed to doing it and they put me up in the Hilton Hotel. Brenda dropped me and Hannah off at Darlington station and I made my way south. I was quietly confident to begin with, and all went well until we arrived at Birmingham station. But then I realised I had no idea where to go at that point. Fortunately, Guide Dogs had arranged for someone to meet me and drive me to the Hilton. The next day, at lunchtime, the talk lasted about 30 minutes and then I was away on my home journey that afternoon. I was booked on the 15.55 p.m. train. A taxi took us to the station and then the problems started. My first worry was, where's the platform? The little I could see didn't really help. All that I could make out in front of me were escalators. Anyone reading this from Birmingham will know where the platforms are: they're on the level below ground level. But I didn't know that. I'm now pushed for time and panicking a bit, particularly as guide dogs don't do escalators. Anyway, to my relief I thought I could see a railway information desk and headed for that. I'm a good asker, so I say to the guy behind the glass, "I hope you don't mind, but I'm with my guide dog and trying to catch a train to Darlington. I think I need help otherwise I'm going to miss it."

The guy was fantastic. He came out and off we went in the lift. When we arrived on the platform there wasn't much space. It was a Friday afternoon so the platform was absolutely heaving with people. With no peripheral vision it was frightening, particularly as everyone started moving as the train was approaching. Without that guy next to me I'm certain I couldn't have coped, but just as the train came to a stop he shouted above the noise, "Ladies and gentlemen - can you step aside please for this gentleman and his guide dog."

Well it was like Moses parting the Red Sea! They left a clear path for me to get on that train and not one single passenger got on until the railway man had settled me in my seat. People are generally very kind.

In my experience, Joe public is very respectful of guide dogs. People will generally ask, "Can I stroke her?"

Most people seem to know that when a dog has a harness on they are in work mode. Perhaps I'm softer than most, but in those situations I just drop the harness and let people make a fuss of her. Obviously, I wouldn't do that when I'm working her. I do remember touching someone's guide dog myself once when the owner, who was totally blind by the way, sensed I'd done that and said, "I'd rather you didn't touch my dog - it's working" in a very fierce voice.

I remembered that incident when I first got Hannah and vowed not to be rude to people if they wanted to make contact with her.

Travelling on the London Underground can be hairy. I've done the same route on the Victoria Line more than once, but I can't begin to attempt that journey without the assistance of strangers. As a rule, famously, people don't talk to one another on the tube. There is very little conversation amongst strangers. If you've got a guide dog you chat to everyone. I have an idea how many stops it is from King's Cross to Vauxhall station, but you have to ask for reassurance. Just as arriving at King's Cross mainline station you need to get guided to a lift. And then, Hannah doesn't know where the Victoria Line is! So, it's all about asking.

And I meet some lovely people as a result.

Once, when Brenda had joined Hannah and I on a trip to London, a woman sat down next to me on the tube; she was from Brazil. Immediately she reacted, "I love your dog. I love your dog!" she repeated.

All that journey, from King's Cross to Vauxhall, Brenda and I were talking to her as if we'd known her forever. As she got up to leave the train I asked her to hold her hand out and I gave her a dog biscuit. She gave it to Hannah and it absolutely made her day.

I speak to more people these days than I have ever spoken to in my life. Guide dogs attract people.

When we are in London, imagine how disorientating that wind is that blows around the tube stations, not to mention the noise of the trains as they rush into a platform. My first big test in London was when Queens Park Rangers invited me back to a game at home to Brighton. And I thought, 'Bloody hell, that's a big ask for Hannah and me.' I had already taken her to a game at Middlesbrough, but that had been a trip where we had been accompanied by Guide Dogs mobility instructor Clare Tansley, and Brenda was with me too. That day, Hannah sat in the stand and she was brilliant. But when QPR asked me down they made it clear they wanted me to go on to the pitch at half-time.

Well, it was around the time I was beginning to organise fundraising for guide dogs and I decided to go because I knew it would help the cause. Anyway, we made the journey south and I remember my biggest fear when we arrived at Loftus Road was whether Hannah might do her ablutions on the pitch! I had a number of poo bags with me that day just in case. As it was, I needn't have worried. She behaved impeccably.

The crowd were great and gave me a lovely ovation, and all the time Hannah never batted an eyelid and just sat and watched. Another emotional moment in my life I will never forget.

I could not quite believe the generosity of people. Wayne Fereday, one of the QPR players, came up to me after the game and gave me some really great news. Apparently, Wayne was at the hairdresser where he lived on the south coast and had got chatting that day with a guy called Tony Perkins, who wanted to get in touch with me about naming a guide-dog puppy with a decent donation. Wayne duly obliged and put Tony - who was a lifelong QPR fan who had watched me play as a kid - in touch with me.

One evening the phone rang and it was Tony. He came straight to the point. "I'd like to donate a little bit of money to your project," he said.

"I understand if an individual raises a certain amount you get to name a guide-dog puppy." Tony was right - but the story was, you had to raise £5,000 for a puppy.

Well, it turned out that Tony's aunt had passed away recently and he said, "I want to name a puppy in memory of my aunt who was called Faith."

I'd imagined, as the amount we'd raised up to this point was just below £30,000, he might make a donation to take it up to that amount by paying a couple of hundred pounds.

Imagine my surprise when, after a pause, he said, "I'd like to give you £10,000 if that helps."

How can anyone give £10,000 of their own money? It just beggars belief. I was stunned and so grateful. Tony had recently been a beneficiary in his auntie's will and he had generously thought this was a great way to remember her. He ended up naming two dogs - the first of which was called Faith after his auntie, and happily Tony actually got to meet the puppy.

Hannah has given me so much, so it's been wonderful to think that through her I can help to give something back to the organisation that has made such a difference to my life.

After all this praise, I wouldn't want you to get the wrong impression. Hannah is no saint!

She can be a bit naughty and she can eat for England, but when she's working she's on it. As soon as that harness goes on she's disciplined and alert. What makes Hannah so special is her ability to cope with country and city life. Dealing with livestock and crowds of people are very different skills that very, very few guide dogs need to be trained for. And just like any of us, she sometimes needs to go to the toilet when we are on a trip away from home and in unfamiliar territory. When we are in town I know immediately when that moment comes because she'll slow her walking pace and eventually head for the kerb. I can just about cope with that with the little vision I have and my little black poo bag. Thankfully, for me and any totally blind person, we'd never get fined if our guide dog fouled the pavement. Guide dogs are rightly exempt from prosecution.

With Hannah I have a level of independence, I can achieve quite a lot and feel safe. It might sound simple, but with a guide dog by your side you never have to worry about people bumping into you. They can see Hannah.

Nothing fazes me. Hannah's given me massive confidence. She's been a lifeline.

CHAPTER 21
These Days...

As I've already said, my week is dictated by the routines essential when you have a guide dog. Most days I'll get out for a jog. Obviously, it has to be a very familiar route, so I'm very aware of where I am running. I take my little white cane with me. That's mostly so people understand my vision is impaired.

A white cane is essential. Here's an example why. Once, before I had a guide dog, I went to the airport, and while being assisted on to the plane two guys came up to me and said, "Where do you think you are going?" - thinking I was jumping the queue. So, I reached for my wallet and showed them my registered blind card. Obviously, they were very embarrassed. Now I don't ever go anywhere without my white cane.

People look out for me. There's a lady locally, Ann Dent, who walks the same disused railway track I use for jogging who always carries a pair of secateurs in her pocket. If she sees any overhanging branch, she'll cut it back. I had a nasty experience with a branch quite recently. I was cutting my grass on a sit-on mower. I drove into an overhanging branch and shredded my face quite badly. But I love my jog round the estate and I'm safe in the knowledge that Brenda is always at home when I'm out for my run. I should always carry my mobile with me, but I don't. It's something Brenda is always badgering me about.

You may be surprised to discover that I still try to manage to play golf. Of course, when I tee off, I have to have my friends behind me! My central vision allows me to see the ball with my head down, but as soon as I hit the ball I have no idea where it's gone.

I don't know at what speed my vision is deteriorating so I just enjoy my jogging and a little bit of golf from time to time as much as possible.

Fly fishing is more of a challenge these days, but I'm still passionate enough to try. Since being registered blind I have been salmon fishing in Scotland, and when I get the chance I still love to fish locally in County Durham. If somebody places me in the river and I'm careful, it's something I'll keep doing as long as I can.

And I've never lost my love of music and more specifically the piano. I can read music a little, but I'm getting more like Stevie Wonder every week! Those lessons from Miss Heslop when I was a kid came in handy. I play almost every day at home and really enjoy it. Recently I was at St. Pancras station in London, where they have a public piano for anyone to play. I'm sure Hannah wondered what the heck was going on when I sat her down and started playing to the crowds of travellers around me.

***

My sight still enables me to watch football a little bit on TV. We are just blessed at the moment as football fans to be around to be able to see two of the greatest players ever, in my opinion. Recently I discovered that ITV4 were showing Real Betis v Barcelona in La Liga, so I tuned in and watched Lionel Messi scoring a hat-trick. It's not often that you see the opposition supporters bowing to an opponent. The hat-trick comprised of a free kick, interlinking play with Luis Suárez for the second, and his third goal was just amazing. He pretended to shoot from outside the box then chipped the goalkeeper. Unbelievable. For me, when it comes to Ronaldo and Messi you can't really compare them. I think it was Rio Ferdinand who summed it up best, when he said that we just have to accept that they are different players, but each is world class in their own way. On goal-scoring alone, they are special. Thirty goals a season consistently for over a decade isn't bad, is it?

Ronaldo is a powerhouse of a player. Wonderful in the air. I saw Ronaldo playing for Juventus recently against Atlético Madrid and he ended up scoring a hat-trick as they came back from two-nil down in the first leg to win a Champions League tie. What an athlete. When he jumps to head the ball in the penalty area he's as high as the crossbar!

Then you have Messi, who is five foot whatever and all that natural ability. He just shades it for me with his dribbling skills and first touch. And both he and Ronaldo perform at that high standard week in week out. Let's not forget the number of assists they wrack up in a season. And they don't seem to get injured and miss games either.

The sad thing is the Argentina national team have never seen the best of Messi. He's a footballing genius, but he's never had the national team success of Maradona or Pelé to back up his club performances. Not Messi's fault. You are only as good as the players around you. Perhaps if Messi were playing for Accrington Stanley he wouldn't score 30 in a season. But I don't think I've ever seen anyone as good as Messi. George Best was up there with the best - even Pelé said that - for five years, but Messi has been God's gift to football.

I still attend the odd live football match here and there. A recent trip to watch Pep Guardiola's Manchester City take on Cardiff City was a wonderful experience for me. I went along to the game with Hannah and my son-in-law. The first person who greeted us was City legend Mike Summerbee, who is an ambassador for the club at home games. I'd picked the right game to see. That night I met up with ex-City players Joe Corrigan, Peter Barnes, Tony Book and even Colin Bell, who I had played with in the England team all those years ago. Mike Summerbee was brilliant. He took us over to the main stand, up in the lift, and into the executive box. Everyone around us wanted to find out more about Hannah, who was clearly the star attraction. When we stepped outside to take our seats for the game, the staff there put a blanket down for Hannah. City won three-nil so everyone around us was happy.

As I left the Etihad, I had to make arrangements for Hannah to do a poo. So, I asked Matt, my son-in-law, to find us a patch of grass. Hannah had been inside the stadium for around five hours so was ready! We found a suitable spot and I managed to pick up what she'd done in a poo bag. Just as I was walking back to Matt's car by the kerb, I told Hannah to go forward. She hesitated as a car pulled out in front of me. There I am with my poo bag as the driver of the car lowers the window and I recognise another City legend, Dennis Tueart, immediately. Again, someone I hadn't seen for years and years and we chatted - mostly about Hannah it has to be said - before we eventually left the stadium after a wonderful night. When us players get together you forget how much you miss that special camaraderie. The buzz I got from meeting all those guys that night was as good as watching the match for me. A special day.

Through football I have made so many wonderful friends down the years. Sad to say, one way in which footballers keep in touch these days is through funerals. One in particular I remember really well was Ray Harford's funeral in 2003. What a turn-out. All the game's great players and coaches seemed to attend. He was a very popular man. Assistant to Kenny Dalglish when Blackburn Rovers won the Premier League in 1995, he was one of the top coaches of his generation. I'd shared a room with Ray when we played in the pro footballers golf tournament once in La Manga. We got on so well. We were like brothers. Sir Alex Ferguson, Alan Shearer, Kenny Dalglish, Terry Venables and Harry Redknapp were among the 300 mourners at Ray's funeral. It was the first time I'd ever met Harry Redknapp apart from on the football field. We got chatting and now we are good friends. He got Brenda and I tickets to go and watch Pompey during his successful time managing them and has been a committed supporter of my Guide Dogs fundraising.

Although it has slowed down a bit now, we have so far raised more than £70,000 for Guide Dogs through my Just Giving page and through generous individual donations. Sky Sports were the catalyst. They sent Dickie Davis to do a filmed interview with me at home. What followed were features on the BBC's *Look North* and ITV, but it was Sky Sports that really helped to spread awareness about what I was attempting to do. The *Soccer Saturday* team all watched my interview: host Jeff Stelling along with Matt Le Tissier, Phil Thompson, Charlie Nicholas and Paul Merson. Interest rocketed as a result.

Once people heard my story, I couldn't have had better support. When I was having my essential white-cane training, Dave Waterfall Brown took me up to the Newcastle Guide Dogs office, where I met Kyla McVicar and Pippa Turner. I wanted to talk over an idea I'd had. This was in 2016, the year before I was lucky enough to get Hannah.

The plan was an ambitious one and Brenda and I collected every Premier League football shirt, signed by the players, to auction off for Guide Dogs. The auction day was at a place called Tennants in Leyburn, North Yorkshire, and it was a big success. Tennants, I should add, didn't charge a penny in commission, which wouldn't have been the case with a well-known London auction house Pippa had contacted. The shirts raised thousands and the top bid for any of them went to the Leicester City signed shirt. Leicester had been crowned Premier League champions before the auction, so that particular shirt attracted a lot of attention. Probably one hell of an investment to the person who bagged that one.

I'd used all my contacts to complete the set of signed shirts, only drawing a blank to begin with at Watford and Liverpool. There weren't many hiccups. Most clubs responded positively and quickly. I left a message with a guy at Watford who said he'd see in to it but never rang me back. Next time I rang I spoke to a receptionist at the club and explained the situation. Whoever she was, she was absolutely brilliant. Well, it turned out her mother was blind and she told me not to worry as she knew where to lay her hands on a signed shirt. She rang me back the next morning to tell me it's in the post. Wonderful.

Liverpool was a frustrating one. I rang the Liverpool FC Foundation and they put me through to someone and I did my usual request and explained I was on the list for a guide dog and raising funds for the guide dogs charity the best way I knew how. Could they send me a signed Liverpool shirt for the big auction to raise money? There was some hesitation at the outset from the woman on the other end of the phone. She explained the procedure for such requests, which they obviously get quite often. And I agreed with her - they clearly received many worthy requests, but not quite like mine, surely. It's the price of the fame of being such a popular football club. I wasn't giving up, though! I persevered and probably didn't do my cause much good by telling her I used to play across the city for Everton. Anyway, she wasn't budging, saying she wanted an email with the request in writing, which we duly did. Then we waited. And waited. Nothing... Well, I'm a bit like a dog with a bone when it comes to these sort of things and I wasn't going to give this one up, so I rang her again. I'm admittedly a bit agitated on the phone and I say, "What's the hold up? What's taking you so long?"

"We haven't made a decision yet," she replies.

To which I reply, losing my patience, "Why do I need a decision when all the other clubs have been so generous getting shirts out to me in 48 hours?"

Anyway, I did have to wait for their decision, which duly arrived in an email.

It said, "A decision has been made to send you a signed Liverpool shirt for the Guide Dogs fund, but before we release it can you please send £7.50 to cover postage?"

Well, you can imagine on reading this that there was steam coming out of my ears!

I ring up the same person at Liverpool and I go ballistic.

"We've just received your email," I say, "and I can tell you now, I'm not going to give in on this. You expect me, as an ex-footballer waiting for a guide dog and raising funds for the charity, to pay £7.50 for postage to get the shirt? If you do that your football club will get the worst publicity in the press you can imagine."

Within a second, she responds by saying, "Well on this occasion we will send the shirt free of charge."

"Thank you very much!" is all I say and I put the phone down. Unbelievable.

The shirt auction may have been the biggest of the fundraising schemes, but the money poured in from a variety of other sources. There was a very generous man called Eamonn Elliott, who offered to run a golf day at Rockliff Hall near Darlington, a wonderful course offered free of charge, and we raised £4,000. Among the prizes donated and auctioned off that day were four bottles of the most incredible whisky from the Angus Dundee distillery, courtesy of lifelong QPR supporter Tania Hillman. Burnley Football Club raised £7,000 when they hosted a dinner to celebrate the 50th anniversary of our lads winning the FA Youth Cup. And my old Burnley team-mate and friend Steve Kindon, who as everyone knows is one of the best after-dinner speakers on the circuit, put on a great show for me during two events - one at Wolves, where my former team-mates turned out to help raise money, and a second up in Chester-le-Street. That brought in another three- or four-thousand pounds. Steve's mate and fellow stand-up comedian Gary Marshall also pulled out all the stops with a couple of fundraising gigs of his own. The Everton Foundation donated £1,000, a figure matched by Manchester United's former players. QPR named a guide dog and a lot of my former pupils in Chichester were very generous.

One of those particular donations came from a lad called Joel Ward, who currently plays for Crystal Palace.

Of all the individuals who helped and supported my cause, a special mention must go to the ever-generous Harry Redknapp, who handed me a very substantial donation.

I'm continuing to raise what money I can for Guide Dogs and thank you for *your* contribution. By buying and reading this book you have added to the fund. All my proceeds from it will help someone like me who dared to hope that one day they might be paired with a dog like Hannah.

POSTSCRIPT

I've talked a good deal about just how much of a lifeline a guide dog can be to someone like me. Here's one final illustration - if one were needed.

Just as we were completing work on this book, Hannah developed a lump on the inside of her back leg. At first it didn't seem to affect her too much and we had the advice that it was probably an allergic reaction to a bite. But the lump grew rapidly and, when she returned to the vet, Hannah had an operation to remove a sizeable abscess, which burst internally. At the same time I went ahead with a public-speaking engagement at nearby Barnard Castle Cricket Club in aid of a men's mental health charity, but without Hannah. Cricketing legend Ian Botham and I were booked as a duo for an audience Q&A and I can tell you I struggled to cope that night. The place was packed, and without Hannah all I had to indicate I was blind was my long white stick that I hadn't used in two-and-a-half years. The number of people at the event was so overwhelming that my friend Roy had to guide me safely to the stage, but not before I had stepped outside to tell myself, "Come on - you can do this."

I nearly didn't. Worrying about Hannah, who was still at the vet's, had put me in an anxious state to begin with. The feeling I had that night reminded me so much of the meltdown I had experienced all those years earlier at Epsom racecourse before being paired with Hannah.

Thankfully, Hannah is now making a full recovery from her operation.

How I would struggle without her.

THE DAVE THOMAS XI

Dave has selected his best eleven players from those he has played with and against during his career. There's one exception: "A lad from the north-east I just couldn't leave out!"

Goalkeeper
GORDON BANKS
In my era we had Ray Clemence, Peter Shilton and Phil Parkes - all great 'keepers - but Gordon, aside from being a World Cup winner, eclipsed all of them with some of the famous saves he made.

Full-back
PAUL REANEY
He always gave me a tough time. Very adventurous and very quick going forward.

Centre-back
FRANK McLINTOCK
The best pro I ever worked with. A real tough leader of men and the best captain I played under. He didn't just think about his own game, he thought a lot about what his team-mates were doing.

Centre-back
BOBBY MOORE
He had a real presence about him. Never seemed to need to hurry. Made all England proud that day in July 1966.

Full-back
RAY WILSON
Lightning-quick over five or ten yards. You could knock the ball past him, but not many got past him to use that ball.

Midfield
PAUL GASCOIGNE
One of the best midfield players in my lifetime, even if he was an absolute idiot! Skilful, strong on the ball, competitive, and he had that rare talent for going past players.

Midfield
BOBBY CHARLTON
Bobby had that aura of gracefulness. He seemed to float across the ground. He played two-footed and his long passes and long-range shooting were out of this world.

Midfield
JOHNNY GILES
Kept things moving and ticking over brilliantly. The master of the passing game.

Striker
JIMMY GREAVES
'Mr Cool' and the best finisher I ever witnessed at first hand. I could have gone for Stan Bowles, but 'Greavsie' did the business of scoring goals for so many seasons. He was a notch above the rest.

THE DAVE THOMAS XI

Striker
BOB LATCHFORD

I assure you, this isn't anything to do with the old pal's act, but he is a really good friend of mine and the perfect No.9. Inside the box he came alive. He had that knack of scoring in so many ways - scruffy goals, off his backside, off his knee. A bit like the German striker Gerd Müller.

Striker
GEORGE BEST

My idol, and a genius in my opinion. The greatest player I have ever seen. Uncoachable, very strong-willed. That's why Matt Busby got the best out of him because he didn't try to tell him to do things in a match he could already do better than anyone. Born with an incredible natural talent.

Manager/Coach
DAVE SEXTON

The most respected man in football.
Dave would have worked for nothing.

Changing lives every day

GUIDE DOGS

Our ambition is for a future where every person with sight loss has the confidence and support to live their lives to the full.

If you have sight loss and need advice about how we might help you, or if you would like to volunteer with Guide Dogs or donate, please contact us:

 **guidedogs.org.uk**

 **info@guidedogs.org.uk**

A charity registered in England and Wales (209617) and Scotland (SC038979). J0324 06/19

Dave Thomas and Hornet Books would like to express grateful thanks to the Professional Footballers' Association for their support in the making of this book and their generous donation to the Guide Dogs charity.

*This book is also available as an ebook
and in formats for blind and partially sighted readers.
Contact Hornet Books for further details.*

info@hornetbooks.com

INDEX

A

Adamson, Dave, 184, 185

Adamson, Jimmy, 40, 49, 52, 55, 57, 59, 64, 102, 103, 104, 184, 185

Agüero, Sergio, 78

Allen, Les, 159

Allison, Malcolm, 64, 88

Anderson, Stan, 90

Angus, John, 26, 38, 51

Armstrong, George, 51

Astle, Jeff, 40

Atkinson, Ron, 56

B

Bailey, Mr, 27

Bainbridge, Sid, 16

Ball, Alan, 25, 38, 39, 61, 97, 159

Ball, Alan (Senior), 38

Banks, Gordon, 207

Barker, Richie, 85, 138, 139, 140

Barnes, John, 167

Barnes, Peter, 51

Barnwell, John, 43, 85, 133, 135, 137, 138, 139, 140, 144

Baxter, Jim, 43

Beardsley, Peter, 145

Beckenbauer, Franz, 98, 147

Beckham, David, 132

Bell, Colin, 198

Bell, Norman, 140

Bell, Sue, 140

Bellamy, Arthur, 40

Best, George, 39, 44, 49, 50, 83, 198, 209

Biley, Alan, 159

Bingham, Billy, 127

Blackbell, Brenda, 56

Blant, Colin, 38

Blockley, Jeff, 41

Bond, Kevin, 139

Bonetti, Peter, 50

Book, Tony, 198

Boonham, Nigel, 14

Botham, Ian, 205

Boulton, Colin, 111, 144, 145

Bowles, Stan, 64, 65, 70, 74, 82, 86, 90, 91, 93, 102, 105, 106, 107, 111, 208

Bradley, 'Dai', 12

Bray, Jack, 86

Bremner, Billy, 81, 112

Bridgwater, Peter, 144, 151, 152

Brooking, Trevor, 44

Brown, Tony, 40

Brown, Willie, 41

Burridge, John, 61

Burtenshaw, Steve, 79, 90, 133
Busby, Martyn, 65
Busby, Sir Matt, 209
Butterfield, Jack, 36

C

Callaghan, Ian, 46
Campbell, Bobby, 65, 156, 158, 159
Campbell, Sol, 170
Carr, Willie, 41, 133
Carter, Philip, 126, 132
Case, Jimmy, 169
Casper, Billy, 12
Channon, Mick, 95, 97
Charlton, Bobby, 39, 44, 94, 208
Charlton, Jack, 81
Charlton, Mr, 26
Clarke, Alison, 171
Clarke, Allan, 96
Clemence, Ray, 97, 207
Clement, Dave, 82, 107, 111
Cliff, Eddie, 41
Clough, Brian, 18, 19, 51, 59, 88, 90, 122
Coates, Ralph, 26, 43, 52, 62
Cocker, Les, 97
Collins, Miss, 16
Connelly, John, 46
Coppell, Steve, 51
Coppock, George, 41
Corrigan, Joe, 198

Crouch, Peter, 170
Currie, Tony, 47
Cushing, Peter, 20

D

Daniels, Mick, 66
Davis, Dickie, 199
Deacon, John, 157, 160, 161
Dean, Dixie, 123
Defoe, Jermain, 170
Dent, Ann, 195
Ditchburn, Jack, 68, 144, 152
Dixon, Lee, 167
Dobson, Martin, 95
Docherty, Mick, 36, 41
Docherty, Tommy, 36, 51, 82, 119, 120
Don, Monty, 89
Dougan, Derek, 57, 88

E

Eastoe, Peter, 119
Edmondson, Walter and Winnie, 36, 37
Eisner, Michael, 170
Elder, Alex, 38
Elliott, Eamonn, 202
Ellis, Doug, 120
England, Mike, 52
Eusébio, 32

INDEX

F

Fereday, Wayne, 192
Ferguson, Sir Alex, 53, 199
Field, Olive, 177
Finney, Tom, 88
Fletcher, Paul, 62, 84
Francis, Gerry, 64, 73, 82, 86, 93, 97, 111, 112, 118
Fresco, Monte, 96
Furphy, Ken, 84

G

Gascoigne, Paul, 208
Gaydamak, Alexandre, 169
Gemmill, Archie, 111
George, Charlie, 111
Gibson, Hilary, 171
Gidman, John, 81
Giles, Johnny, 81, 145, 146, 208
Gillard, Ian, 75, 78, 82, 93, 108
Gilliat, Roger, 167
Givens, Don, 75, 82, 83, 86, 112, 119
Gray, Andy, 133, 139
Gray, Eddie, 108
Greaves, Jimmy, 44, 52, 85, 208
Greenwood, Jim, 134
Gregory, Jim, 64, 90, 91, 108, 118, 119
Grobbelaar, Bruce, 144
Guardiola, Pep, 198

H

Haddock, James, 168, 169
Hailey, Jack, 25
Håland, Alf-Inge, 81, 82
Hall, Sir John, 13
Hamilton, Bryan, 129
Hankin, Ray, 145
Hansen, Alan, 128
Harford, Ray, 199
Harris, Gordon, 38
Harris, Ron, 50, 81
Harrison, Eric, 132, 133
Harry the Coat, 74
Hartley, David, 41
Hartley, Mr, 16
Harvey, Colin, 38
Harvey, David, 145
Hateley, Mark, 158
Hawthorne, Nigel, 12
Hazell, John, 133, 134, 135
Healey, Derek, 63
Healy, Tim, 12, 13
Hector, Kevin, 111
Heighway, Steve, 51
Hennessey, Terry, 43
Heslop, Miss, 21, 196
Higgs, Peter, 61
Hill, Gordon, 51
Hill, Jimmy, 88
Hillman, Tania, 202
Hixon, Jack, 26, 27

Hogg, Charlie, 13
Holding, Gerald, 157
Hollins, John, 107, 108, 113
Hood, Peter, 168, 169
Howe, Don, 114
Howe, Ernie, 159
Hudson, Alan, 58, 98, 106
Hughes, Emlyn, 97, 133, 137
Hunter, Norman, 81, 112
Hurst, Geoff, 44, 46

I

Icke, David, 41
Irvine, Willie, 51

J

Jago, Gordon, 63, 64, 65, 69, 70, 79, 90, 91, 105, 107, 156
James, Leighton, 55
Jarvis, Tony, 22
John, Elton, 125
Jones, Ken, 47
Jones, Peter, 37, 41
Jones, Ron, 101
Jordan, Joe, 112

K

Keane, Roy, 81, 82
Keegan, Kevin, 97, 114, 150
Keevil, Helen, 76, 77, 96, 146, 147, 149, 182

Keevil, Teddy, 77
Keevil, Tom, 77
Kelly, Eddie, 119
Kendall, Howard, 150
Kennedy, Ray, 114
Kerr, Bobby, 66, 68
Kerr, Cathy, 66
Keys, Richard, 125
Kidd, Brian, 47, 132
Kindon, Steve, 41, 62, 114, 202
King, Andy, 127, 128
Kirkpatrick, Roger, 60, 61
Knowles, Cyril, 155, 166

L

Lalley, John, 138
Lampard, Frank, 80
Larwood, Harold, 9
Latcham, Les, 38, 49
Latchford, Bob, 84, 122, 123, 127, 132, 133, 209
Laurie, Stuart, 66
Law, Denis, 39, 84
Le Tissier, Matt, 200
Leach, Martin, 125
Leach, Mick, 82, 107, 111
Lee, Francis, 111
Lee, Gordon, 121, 126, 131, 133
Lipton, Sir Thomas, 11, 14
Lloyd, Cliff, 102
Lochhead, Andy, 38, 52

INDEX

Logan, Dr Sue, 175
Long, Roy, 66, 205
Lord, Sir Bob, 31, 53, 54, 57, 59, 61, 62, 103, 104
Lorimer, Peter, 145
Lukic, John, 167

M

Mackay, Dave, 52, 101, 111
Maddox, Albert, 31, 103, 104
Mancini, Terry, 82
Mandaric, Milan, 169
Manders, Rachel, 183, 184
Mansell, Jack, 90
Maradona, Diego, 197
Marsh, Rodney, 64, 90
Marshall, Gary, 202
Masson, Don, 80, 107, 112
Matthews, Stanley, 19
Mayhew, John, 176, 177
Mazzucco, Ralph, 147
Mazzucco, Sharon, 147
McEvoy, Gerry, 41
McFarland, Roy, 111
McGrath, Paul, 53
McGregor, Jim, 126, 131
McIlroy, Jimmy, 52
McKenzie, Duncan, 122, 127
McLintock, Frank, 52, 80, 82, 86, 91, 107, 108, 112, 207
McNee, Keith, 37

McParland Peter, 19
McVicar, Kyla, 200
Mercer, Joe, 83
Merrick, Geoff, 35
Merson, Paul, 200
Messi, Lionel, 48, 197, 198
Miller, Brian, 63
Moore, Bobby, 14, 207
Moore, Brian, 88, 168
Moores, John, 124, 126
Morgan, Phil, 177
Morgan, Willie, 38, 43, 44
Morrissey, Johnny, 51
Motson, John, 88
Müller, Gerd, 209
Murdoch, Bobby, 155
Murray, George, 26

N

Neasom, Mike, 162
Neville, Gary, 132
Neville, Phil, 132
Newton, Henry, 43, 111
Nicholas, Charlie, 200
Nish, David, 59, 111

O

Olive, Les, 134
Oliver, Linda, 182, 183
Oliver, Michael, 130
O'Neil, Brian, 26, 62

O'Rourke, John, 102
Osgood, Peter, 105, 162

P

Paddon, Graham, 41, 160
Paine, Terry, 46, 51, 81
Paisley, Bob, 144
Palance, Jack, 113
Parkes, Phil, 75, 82, 93, 207
Parsons, John 56
Pearce, Jack, 165, 166, 167
Pejic, Mike, 128, 129
Pelé, 32, 57, 147, 197, 198
Perkins, Tony, 192, 193
Peters, Martin, 44
Pilkington, Brian, 52
Pointer, Ray, 52
Potts, Harry, 27, 32, 37, 43, 46, 49, 54, 55, 58
Powell, Jeff, 95
Probert, Eric, 41, 53

Q

Quill, Greg, 198

R

Ramayon, Maureen, 75
Ramayon, Sav, 75
Ramsey, Sir Alf, 46, 47, 50, 58, 83, 85
Reaney, Paul, 81, 127, 207

Redknapp, Harry, 199, 203
Revie, Don, 27, 28, 29, 31, 45, 61, 64, 66, 79, 80, 83, 85, 88, 94, 95, 97
Reynolds, Mr, 29, 30, 31
Richards, John, 133
Rioch, Bruce, 111, 162
Roberts, Richie, 139
Robertson, John, 51
Robson, Bryan, 53
Robson, Jack, 26
Rogers, Alan, 158
Ronaldo, Cristiano, 197
Ross, Harry, 178

S

St John, Ian, 52
Salt, Neil, 22, 23
Sexton, Dave, 38, 39, 87, 93, 101, 105, 107, 108, 109, 117, 120, 121, 134, 135, 176, 209
Shackleton, Granville, 37
Shand, Mr and Mrs, 164, 165
Shankly, Bill, 52, 130, 131, 132, 150
Shankly, Nessie, 131
Shanks, Don, 74, 106, 107, 131
Shearer, Alan, 27, 199
Shilton, Peter, 94, 97, 207
Sibley, Frank, 75, 120
Smith, Fred, 38
Smith, Geoffrey, 89
Smith, Tommy, 52, 81

INDEX

Sparks, Don, 17

Stelling, Jeff, 200

Stepney, Alex, 82

Stokoe, Bob, 66, 69, 70

Storey-Moore, Ian, 43

Strachan, Gordon, 169

Suárez, Luiz, 197

Suart, Ron, 25

Summerbee, Mike, 51, 198

T

Tait, Mick, 159

Tansley, Clare, 184, 188, 191

Taylor, Alan, 145

Taylor, Bill, 97

Taylor, Gordon, 134

Taylor, Graham, 125

Taylor, Jack, 129, 130

Taylor, Michael, 16

Taylor, Peter, 59

Thomas, Brenda, 7, 8, 56, 59, 62, 65, 67, 68, 69, 70, 73, 74, 75, 76, 78, 88, 89, 95, 96, 104, 121, 124, 125, 133, 134, 135, 140, 144, 146, 147, 149, 151, 152, 156, 164, 167, 170, 171, 173, 174, 175, 176, 177, 178, 179, 181, 182, 188, 189, 191, 196, 199, 200

Thomas, Clive, 129

Thomas, David Lloyd (dad), 9, 10, 11, 12, 13, 15, 17, 18, 19, 21, 22, 23, 25, 26, 27, 28, 29, 30, 31, 32, 33, 36, 38, 54, 87, 95, 145, 155, 164

Thomas, David Reece (grandad), 9, 10, 11, 12, 13, 14, 17, 18, 25

Thomas, Jessie (mum), 9, 10, 15, 17, 22, 23, 26, 28, 29, 30, 31, 32, 33, 34, 36, 38, 54, 87, 145, 155

Thomas, Melvin, 10, 25, 28, 29, 30, 95, 145

Thomas, Michael, 166, 167

Thomas, Rod, 111

Thompson, Harold, 103, 104

Thompson, Jimmy, 51

Thompson, Peter, 50, 51

Thompson, Phil, 200

Thomson, Harry, 38, 40

Thrower, Percy, 104, 105

Todd, Colin, 111, 128

Todd, Sam, 38

Trapani, Mark, 169, 170

Tueart, Dennis, 198

Turner, Pippa, 200

Tye, John, 77

U/V

Valentine, Carl, 148

Venables, Terry, 64, 65, 67, 73, 82, 102, 103, 104, 107, 199

W

Waiters, Tony, 143, 150, 151, 152

INDEX

Waldron, Colin, 60

Walker, Keith, 18

Ward, Andre, 86

Ward, Joel, 203

Ward, Mr and Mrs, 21

Warren, Fred, 96

Waterfall Brown, Dave, 183, 185, 200

Waterman, Dennis, 12, 13

Watson, Dave, 97, 99

Watson, Miss, 16

Webb, Dave, 80, 91, 107, 108, 114, 119

Webb, Neil, 159

West, Alan, 41

West, Gordon, 38

Whiteside, Norman, 53

Whitfield, Mr and Mrs, 21

Wilshaw, Dennis, 140

Wilson, James, 77

Wilson, Les, 148

Wilson, Matt, 198

Wilson, Oliver, 77

Wilson, Polly, 76, 77, 146, 147, 149, 177

Wilson, Ray, 208

Wood, George, 121

Worthington, Frank, 48, 95

Wright, Tommy, 38

Wrigley, Wilf, 41

X/Y/Z

Yeats, Ron, 52

Yorath, Peter, 145